*Dedicated to Marjorie Appleton
who has been the companion on
my journey.*

ACKNOWLEDGEMENTS

The author and publishers would like to acknowledge their indebtedness for permission to reproduce copyright material as follows: from *Markings* by Dag Hammarskjöld, published by Faber & Faber Ltd; from *My God*, *My Glory* and *A Procession of Passion Prayers* by Eric Milner-White, published by the SPCK; the poem 'The Living Truth' by Sydney Carter © Stainer Bell Ltd.

The Scripture quotations are from the *Revised Standard Version Bible*, copyrighted 1946, 1952 and © 1971 by the Division of Christian Education of the National Council of the Churches of Christ in the USA and are used by permission.

The author would like to thank his secretary, Jean Waddell, for her invaluable help in the preparation of this book of devotion.

CONTENTS

I. WHO AM I?

1. An Embodied Being   15
2. A Thinking Being   18
3. A Feeling Being   21
4. A Spiritual Being   23
5. A Social Being   26
6. A Being Come of Age   29
7. A Being on the Way   32

II. WHAT OF MY LIFE?

8. Experience   37
9. Enjoyment of the World   39
10. Sleep   42
11. Success and Failure   44
12. Old Age   47
13. Standing up to Life   50
14. Death and Beyond   53

III. WITH WHOM?

15. A Royal Law   59
16. People in Need   61
17. Enemies   64
18. World Citizens   67
19. People of other Faiths   70
20. Open Hearts   73
21. Can I be of any Help?   76

IV. HOW SHALL I LIVE?

22. Become as a Child   81
23. Trust Life   84
24. Seek the Truth   87
25. Love   90
26. Keep Steady   93
27. Integrity   96
28. Serenity   99

V. WHAT OBSTACLES?

29. Self-Evaluation 105
30. Self-Centredness 107
31. Immaturity 110
32. Worry 113
33. Shortfall 115
34. Lack of Faith 118
35. Just Plain Sin 121

VI. IN THE BEGINNING

36. God Himself 127
37. Creator 129
38. God Immanent 132
39. Incarnation 135
40. Indwelling 138
41. Transcendent 141
42. Permeating 144

VII. WHO IS CHRIST?

43. A Vital Question 151
44. Really Man 154
45. His Mind 157
46. The Kingdom 159
47. Ever-present 162
48. The Christ-Community 165
49. Omega Point 168

VIII. THROUGH JESUS CHRIST

50. The Love of the Cross 175
51. Redemption through the Cross 178
52. Liberation through Christ 181
53. Jesus the Healer 184
54. Disturber of our Peace 187
55. King of Saints 190
56. In Debt to Christ 193

IX. INNER SPACE
  57. Communication   199
  58. Prayer   201
  59. Silence   204
  60. Guidance   207
  61. Renewal   209
  62. Resurrection Now   212
  63. Worship   215

X. IN THE END
  64. Time   221
  65. Eternity   224
  66. Judgement   227
  67. Completing the Universe   230
  68. Unceasing Purpose   233
  69. To the End   236
  70. In the End   239

   Index   243

INTRODUCTION

This book of thoughts from the Bible, insights gathered from the readings of many years, prayers of other people which spoke to my own spirit and others which came out of my own spirit, is the product of a long and adventurous life. Twenty years of it were spent in Asia, partly in the villages of the Irrawaddy delta, partly in training young men of Burma to be priests, culminating in three years as Director of Public Relations for the Government of Burma in exile and during the first year of liberation. This was followed by eight years in an ecumenical missionary post which gave me a widening knowledge of the world and the world-wide Church. A period followed in a parish on the frontier between East London and the City of London, with friendships with businessmen on the City side and with many homeless drifting people who still seem to make up White-chapel and Stepney. A short and lovely period at St Paul's Cathedral was followed by an unexpected call to be Archbishop of Perth in a time of great growth in Western Australia, and later an equally unexpected move to be Anglican Archbishop in Jerusalem for five exciting years.

I have got to know people under widely differing conditions of life, people of different races and different religions. I have had to struggle to see the meaning of life and to discern a purpose within it and beyond it. I have had to wrestle with my own nature, my own fears, desires and ambitions, as well as with the difficulties, duties and opportunities of the situations in which I have been involved. I can look back on the journey by which I have reached the point where I now am, and this seems to give me a sense of continuity and direction.

This book also looks at the journey still ahead and in putting it together I have been conscious of a three-directional movement. First of all there has been a journey within, into my own being, trying to discover who and what

I really am. Then there has been an upward look to God, guided by the Bible and other Scriptures, the faith and insights of other people, still more from quiet meditation and intuitive flashes, which suggest Someone behind the scenes, with a greater wisdom, a more stimulating mind and a deeper love than my own. Thirdly there has been an outward movement towards fellow-travellers, wanting to know them more intimately, grateful for their friendship and help, and hoping to be a good companion as we journey together.

After a long life, one inevitably looks to the years that are left and what is to come when the journey moves through the curtain into the life beyond this one.

As will be seen in the list of writers from whom quotations have been gratefully acknowledged, this book owes much to stimulating thoughts and inspiring ideas from writers, preachers and friends. Some have gone down into the store-house of memory without a name attached. Should anyone recognize something which came from him, will he please accept my anonymous gratitude.

I hope that those who use this book will take plenty of time over each section, and not just hurry through as an easy, ready-to-hand substitute for their own reflection, meditation and prayer, though even this may be helpful when mind and spirit are tired. I hope they will let their minds wander and go off at tangents in the stimulation of any thought or prayer, so that their own unrecognized needs may be met, and they too feel in touch with an unseen Companion on their spiritual journey.

Lastly, I hope that there will be times when words are not needed, when thoughts are stilled and the spirit is held silent and loving in the embrace of him from whom we all came, in whom we all live and move and have our being, and who is our final home.

1. WHO AM I?

How can I understand the mystery of my total being?
How explore my inner being?

1. AN EMBODIED BEING

It is as a body that I am most aware of myself, and my strongest and most elemental instincts are directed to satisfy the needs and desires of the body. The body is a wonderful organism – breathing, circulation of the blood, digestion and sewerage, sexual feeling and the capacity for union and the procreation of children. The body has a marked effect on the feeling tone of its owner. It is an integral part of our being; it is basically good because given us by God. It must be the servant of the total personality, through which the person expresses himself in demeanour and behaviour.

INSIGHTS FROM SCRIPTURE

Gratitude for the body
I will give thanks unto thee, for I am fearfully and wonderfully made: marvellous are thy works, and that my soul knoweth right well.   *Psalm 139: 13* (BCP)

Sanctification of the body
I appeal to you therefore, brethren, by the mercies of God, to present your bodies as a living sacrifice, holy and acceptable to God.   *Romans 12: 1*

The Divine takes a human body
In the beginning was the Word, and the Word was with God, and the Word was God . . . And the Word became flesh and dwelt among us, full of grace and truth.
                                                      John 1: 1,14

Transformation needed
I tell you this, brethren: flesh and blood cannot inherit the kingdom of God, nor does the perishable inherit the imperishable.   *1 Corinthians 15: 50*

(He) will change our lowly body to be like his glorious body,
by the power which enables him even to subject all things to
himself.   *Philippians 3:21*

OTHER INSIGHTS

Heredity?
Today we know about chromosomes, the units of heredity
received from our parents. It may soon be possible to
modify biological chromosomes, but this will be an awe-
inspiring responsibility, only safe to be exercised in co-
operation with the Creator, who knows how things went
wrong, and whose will is to have them set right.

Hurting the body and its owner
In every generation men have maltreated and killed the
bodies of their fellow-men. Science and technology have
given us powers to do this on a terrifyingly massive scale,
and also to disrupt and annihilate the whole personality.
The development of our spiritual nature must keep pace
with our technological power, otherwise the devaluation of
man will continue and man's inhumanity to man become
totally destructive.

The body spiritualized
The New Testament promises us that our physical body
shall be transmuted into a spiritualized body, like the body
of the risen Christ, released from the domination of the
material, the spatial and the temporal. Yet in some mysterious way it will be recognizable perhaps with its most
significant features, as the nail-marks and the spear-wound
on our Lord's resurrection body. We may think of the body
as a life-long comrade, who will survive death and in some
spiritualized form be our comrade still.

PRAYERS

Body and soul
O eternal God, who has made all things for man, and man
for thy glory: sanctify our bodies and souls, our thoughts
and our intentions, our words and actions. Let our body be
a servant of our mind, and both body and spirit servants of
Jesus Christ; that doing all things for thy glory here, we
may be partakers of thy glory hereafter; through the same
Jesus Christ our Lord. *Jeremy Taylor*

Wisdom for the body
Grant, O creator Spirit, that in all the discoveries of men of
the secrets of human personality and the workings of the
human body, with its inheritance of chromosomes from
parents and ancestors, we may be guided by thy wisdom and
love and by an ever-deepening reverence and care for our
fellow-men, designed by thee to grow into the maturity of
Jesus Christ, the image of thy divinity and the perfection of
our humanity.

A glorious body
O God, who hast shown us by the resurrection of Jesus
Christ that the whole of man's life shall be redeemed and
transformed. We thank thee that in him our bodies shall be
transformed and glorified as his glorious body. Grant us so
to discipline and use them now that they may more perfectly become the instrument of our spirit, prepared for
eternal life. Through him, who died and was buried and
now lives and reigns with thee in glory, ever our Saviour
Jesus Christ.

Blessed be thou, O God, who hast made my body to be a
temple for thy Holy Spirit.

2. A THINKING BEING

Man is distinguished from the animals by possessing, among other things, a conscious mind, with the ability to think, reason, remember, imagine, understand and express himself. He is not just mind, nor is mind just a machine that he uses. It is a vital part of man's personality but not the whole of it. It needs to be brought under the inspiration and guidance of God.

INSIGHTS FROM SCRIPTURE

The dedicated mind
And you shall love the Lord your God with all your heart, and with all your soul, and with all your mind, and with all your strength.   *Mark 12:30*, cf. Deuteronomy 6:5

The thoughts of the mind
Whatever is true, whatever is honourable, whatever is just, whatever is pure, whatever is lovely, whatever is gracious, if there is any excellence, if there is anything worthy of praise, think about these things.   *Philippians 4:8*

The transformed mind
Do not be conformed to this world but be transformed by the renewal of your mind, that you may prove what is the will of God, what is good and acceptable and perfect.
                    Romans 12:2

The ideal mind
Have this mind among yourselves, which is yours in Christ Jesus.   *Philippians 2:5*

OTHER INSIGHTS

The prototype
The mind of man is meant to be a microcosm of the mind of
God. This was shown supremely, in terms of a human life,
in Jesus Christ. We therefore need to study the records of
that divine and human life, recognizing the faith of the
writers but reaching back as far as possible to the life itself.
Also, by communion with the ever-living, ever-present
Christ, we can experience direct, intuitive contact and
illumination.

Thinking about God
Every man must at times want to interpret his own inner
experience. He must from time to time think about the
source of his life, the beginning and end of things, his own
aspirations and failures, the world in which he lives. In a
way, each man is his own theologian, though he will be
interested in what other men have worked out for themselves, and in the record of men's experience of God recorded
in holy Scripture and in saintly lives.

Consecrating the intellect
The merely intellectual man is proud of his own learning,
living in books, thinking only in abstractions, sure that
everything can be solved in terms of human wisdom, believing that man's chief drawback is ignorance and that as
he grows wiser he must inevitably grow better. He lives for
files, schemes, blueprints, scornful of human relationships
and of the common people who cannot share his scholarship. If the world could have been saved by wisdom it
would have been saved long ago.   *W. R. Inge*

PRAYERS

What is worth knowing
Grant to us, O Lord, to know that which is worth knowing,

to love that which is worth loving, to praise that which pleases thee most, to esteem that which is precious unto thee, and to dislike whatsoever is evil in thy eyes. Grant us with true judgement to distinguish things that differ, and above all to search out and do what is well pleasing to thee, through Jesus Christ our Lord.   *Thomas à Kempis*

Light in dark corners

Penetrate these murky corners where we hide memories, and tendencies on which we do not care to look, but which we will not disinter and yield freely up to you, that you may purify and transmute them. The persistent buried grudge, the half-acknowledged enmity which is still smouldering; the bitterness of that loss we have not turned into sacrifice, the private comfort we cling to, the secret fear of failure which saps our initiative and is really inverted pride; the pessimism which is an insult to your joy. Lord, we bring all these to you, and we review them with shame and penitence in your steadfast light.   *Evelyn Underhill*

A great thinker's prayer

Give me, O Lord, a steadfast heart, which no unworthy thought can drag downwards, an unconquered heart, which no tribulation can wear out; an upright heart, which no unworthy purpose may tempt aside. Bestow upon me also, O Lord my God, understanding to know thee, diligence to seek thee, wisdom to find thee, and a faithfulness that may finally embrace thee; through Jesus Christ our Lord.   *Thomas Aquinas*

O the depth of the riches and wisdom and knowledge of God! How unsearchable are his judgements and how inscrutable his ways! 'For who has known the mind of the Lord, or who has been his counsellor?' 'Or who has given a gift to him that he might be repaid?' For from him and through him and to him are all things. To him be glory for ever. Amen.   *Romans 11 : 33–36*

3. A FEELING BEING

Personal life is made up of thinking, feeling and willing, and all those need due recognition and expression. Most of us were taught to control and sometimes repress our emotions, to give more emphasis to the other two partners of mind and will. But if feeling is starved, our inner life becomes unbalanced and unsatisfied. The trinity of the human personality is of co-equals held together in unity.

INSIGHTS FROM SCRIPTURE

The real source
Out of the heart come evil thoughts, murder, adultery, fornication, theft, false witness, slander. These are what defile a man. *Matthew 15:19–20*

Hidden feelings
The heart knows its own bitterness, and no stranger shares its joy. *Proverbs 14:10*

Fellow feeling
Rejoice with those who rejoice, weep with those who weep. *Romans 12:15*

Not completely hidden
Man looks on the outward appearance, but the Lord looks on the heart. *1 Samuel 16:7*

I am he who searches mind and heart. *Revelation 2:23*

Sanctified feelings
The fruit of the Spirit is love, joy, peace, patience, kindness, goodness, faithfulness, gentleness, self-control.
Galatians 5:22–23

OTHER INSIGHTS

Feelings speak

Feelings indicate more frankly what is going on in the depths of a man's being than his carefully controlled thoughts and words. While some feelings may need to be examined and radically changed, they also need to be recognized as the expression of character and regarded as an integral part of a man's inner nature.

Undeveloped feelings

In my experience . . . the most difficult as well as the most ungrateful persons, apart from habitual liars, are the so-called intellectuals . . . Anything can be settled by an intellect that is not subject to the control of feeling – and yet the intellectual still suffers from a neurosis if feeling is undeveloped.

C. G. Jung

Experiment and intuition

During the height of the discussion of the God-is-dead theology, a psychiatrist friend said to me that Christians must not lose their nerve. He added that he and some of his Freudian colleagues, as a result of treating hundreds of mentally sick people, were coming to believe that there was something autonomous within the human psyche, thus confirming the Christian intuition of faith.

PRAYERS

Inner life

O Lord God, I thank thee for the growing knowledge of myself, of the depths of personality which affect my thinking, my feeling, my behaviour, and my dreams. There is so much more than I ever thought, so much more to offer thee for the cleansing and sanctifying of thy Spirit. Heal my inner divisions in the unity of thy will, set my fears at rest in the assurance of thy love and grace, let no resentments destroy my inner peace, no thoughts of self deflect me from thy purpose for me. Help me to grow towards the fullness of life and love seen in thy blessed Son, Jesus Christ my Lord.

The divine Spirit in the human spirit
O Spirit of God who dost speak to spirits created in thine own likeness: penetrate into the depths of our spirits, into the storehouse of memories remembered and forgotten, into the depths of being, the very springs of personality. And cleanse and forgive, making us whole and holy, that we may be thine and live in the new being of Christ our Lord.

Known as I am known
O thou to whom all hearts are open, cleanse the thoughts of my heart. O thou to whom all desires are known, purify my desires. O thou to whom no secrets are hid, make known to me my inner life. Strengthen me to grow into that divine likeness which thou didst plant in me at my creation, that my feelings may rise from love and holiness, and my thoughts be governed by truth, O Creator God, redeeming Lord and sanctifying Spirit.

God, examine me and know my heart, probe me and know my thoughts; make sure I do not follow pernicious ways, and guide me in the way that is everlasting.

Psalm 139: 23–24
(Jerusalem Bible)

4. A SPIRITUAL BEING

When we talk of 'spirit' in man, we are pointing to that extra dimension of being that belongs to him and that makes him more than a mere physical organism or a highly complicated animal.   *John Macquarrie*

INSIGHTS FROM SCRIPTURE

Like God
God created man in his own image . . . male and female he
created them. And God blessed them.   *Genesis 1 : 27–28*

. . . the Lord God formed man of dust from the ground, and
breathed into his nostrils the breath of life; and man became a living being.   *Genesis 2 : 7*

Partakers of the divine nature.   *2 Peter 1 : 4*

His own name
. . . I will give him a white stone, with a new name written
on the stone which no one knows except him who receives
it.   *Revelation 2 : 17*

Deep down within
Out of the depths I cry to thee, O Lord!   *Psalm 130 : 1*

OTHER INSIGHTS

What is the self?
There is a spirit in the soul, untouched by time and flesh,
flowing from the spirit, remaining in the spirit, itself wholly
spiritual. In this principle is God, ever verdant, ever flowing
in all the joy and glory of his actual self. Sometimes I have
called that principle the Tabernacle of the soul, sometimes
a spiritual Light, anon I say it is a Spark. But now I say it is
more exalted over this and that than the heavens are exalted
above the earth. So now I name it in a nobler fashion . . .
It is free of all names, and void of all forms. It is one and
simple as God is one and simple, and no man can in any
wise behold it.   *Meister Eckhart*

What would survive?
The one fundamental problem is what we should still
possess if the whole of our world were destroyed tomorrow

and we stood naked before God. The eschatological belief crudely and ruthlessly sweeps away our little moral business, strips us naked of worldly possessions and asks what survives the catastrophe.   *E. C. Hoskyns*

Being myself
If a man begins to observe not only his behaviour, but the mainspring of his actions he will be surprised to find that for hours, days, years, decades, with occasional interruptions, he is no conscious actor, but a puppet well- or ill-behaved, and that the sum of moments when he knows himself to exist is very small indeed.   *C. de Masirerich*

PRAYERS

A soul to make
Thou hast given me a soul to make; make thou it for me, and build me into thy spiritual temple, for Jesus' sake.
W. R. Matthews

Christ within
O Christ my Lord, I pray that you will turn my heart to you in the depths of my being, where with the noise of creatures silenced and the clamour of bothersome thoughts stilled, I shall stay with you, where I find you always present and when I love and worship you.
Fr Lessius, SJ

In the depths
Help me, O Lord, to descend into the depths of my being, below my conscious and sub-conscious life until I discover my real self, that which is given me from thee, the divine likeness in which I am made and into which I am to grow, the place where your Spirit communes with mine, the spring from which all my life rises.

Blessed be thou, O God, who alone can say I AM in thine own right. Blessed be thou, O God, from whom I derive, and in whom I too can say 'I am'.

5. A SOCIAL BEING

We cannot imagine a human being living from birth without any contact with fellow-men. Without other people we could not achieve worthwhile self-consciousness. Human personality cannot develop in isolation. Human society cannot function without understanding, communication and co-operation between people. I *am* only through relationship with others.

INSIGHTS FROM SCRIPTURE

Man needs companions
It is not good that the man should be alone; I will make him a helper fit for him. *Genesis 2:18*

We . . . are . . . individually members one of another.
Romans 12:5

A closer relationship
For just as the body is one and has many members, and all the members of the body, though many, are one body, so it is with Christ. *1 Corinthians 12:12*

Everything made for man
The sabbath was made for man, not man for the sabbath.
Mark 2:27

Infinitely precious
The brother for whom Christ died.
1 Corinthians 8:11

OTHER INSIGHTS

True relationship with others
True relationship with others involves humility of attitude,

refusal to treat others as things or slaves, refusal to pass judgement upon them, acceptance of their limitations and culpability, readiness to welcome and to listen to what they have to say, respect for their uniqueness, progressive understanding of their mystery, trust in what they can become, stimulation of their spiritual progress, appreciation of both the value and insufficiency of ethical norms and moral virtues. *Emile Rideau*

The essence of man
The individual man himself does not have the essence of man in himself as a moral or a thinking being. The essence of man is found only in the community, in the unity of man with man. *Ludwig Feuerbach*

Encounter with others
In the world of encounter you do not know in advance what the other person is going to say or what demand he will make on you. That lies entirely outside your own control. When he speaks, you have to respond – to commit yourself. That is something quite different from being in command of the situation and being yourself the judge. In the way you respond you yourself come under judgement; it reveals the kind of person you are. *J. H. Oldham*

Two dangers
The first is that a man lives for himself alone, deciding everything in the light of his own advantage, disregarding the rights and needs of his fellow-men. The second is that we should think of people impersonally, in the mass, with numbers rather than names, thinking of them as cast in the same mould, with no individuality of their own. Each man wants value in himself, wants to be himself, thinking of others in the same way. Neither individualism nor collectivism is the right way of human relationship.

PRAYERS

Bound together
O God, who hast bound us together in this bundle of life, give us grace to understand how our lives depend upon the courage, the industry, the honesty, and the integrity of our fellow-men; that we may be mindful of their needs, grateful for their faithfulness, and faithful in our responsibilities to them; through Jesus Christ our Lord.   *Reinhold Niebuhr*

An understanding heart
Grant me, O Lord, an understanding heart, that I may see into the hearts of thy people, and know their strengths and weaknesses, their hopes and despairs, their efforts and failures, their need of love and their need to love. Through my touch with them grant comfort and hope, and the assurance that new life begins at any age and on any day, redeeming the past, sanctifying the present, and brightening the future with the assurance of thy unfailing love, brought to me in Jesus Christ, thy Son, my Lord.

'Isness' and becoming
O Creator Lord, let me feel the 'isness' of things and people, without resistance, without trying to impose my own pattern upon them or exploit them for selfish ends. Let me welcome them, enjoy them, value them, love them, for what they are and for what they are becoming through your creative love.

The radiating prayer
[Beginning from within the heart, and sending out to those near to us, then in widening circles to others in our village or town, to those of our own nation, then neighbouring nations, till finally the whole of mankind, living and departed, is reached in the radiation in turn of goodwill, compassion, love, joy, peace, blessing, remembering that

these lovely dispositions start from God within ourselves and are reinforced by his infinitely more generous radiation.]

Blessing to all
Now may every living thing, young or old, weak or strong, living near or far, known or unknown, living or departed or yet unborn, may every living thing be full of bliss.

The Buddha

6. A BEING COME OF AGE

One of the insights or claims of our modern era is that man has come of age and has accepted responsibility for himself and his environment. He is no longer at the mercy of circumstances. Rivers can be diverted or dammed, mountains can be levelled, deserts irrigated, epidemics prevented. He can circle the earth and land on the planets. He is tempted to think that he is all-sufficient, that he has no need to depend on higher powers. He hopes to postpone death and thinks he can do without God.

INSIGHTS FROM SCRIPTURE

A God-given authority
Be fruitful and multiply, and fill the earth and subdue it; and have dominion . . . over every living thing that moves upon the earth. *Genesis 1:28*

The world at his feet
What is man that you have been mindful of him,
Mortal man that you have taken note of him,
That you have made him little less than divine
And adorned him with glory and majesty;
You have made him master over your handiwork,
Laying the world at his feet? *Psalm 8:5–7*
(from a Jewish translation)

An early assessment
This is only the beginning of what they will do; and nothing
that they propose to do will now be impossible for them.
Genesis 11:6

The ultimate goal
Until we all attain to the unity of the faith and of the knowledge of the Son of God, to mature manhood, to the measure
of the stature of the fullness of Christ.   *Ephesians 4:13*

OTHER INSIGHTS

The paradox of man
Modern man can fly at a speed faster than sound, can communicate by radio to every part of the world in the fraction
of a second, can circle the earth and land on the moon, and
descend to the depths of the sea. He can make nuclear
weapons and biological warfare. Modern man has learned
how to control births; he may soon be able to determine sex,
and possibly to intervene in the working of chromosomes.
Yet what a mess he has made of the world – wars, slums,
hunger, racial prejudice, refugees, pollution!

Modern man's idea of himself
Man has come of age. He rejects the Christian teachings. He
is not sinful; he is good, and responsible for himself; he
deserves liberty, the right of self-expression, and will no
longer be restrained and subdued by life-hating supersti-
tions, nor will he live as a pitiful weakling, craving for grace
which he is supposed not to merit. He is independent and
stands on his own. He will neither be damned nor treated
with compassion.   *Professor J. L. Talmon*
                    (at the Jerusalem Colloquium on Religion,
                Peoplehood, Nation and Land, November 1970)

Spiritual maturity?
Man has grown greatly in knowledge of the universe and in
discovery of the laws by which it works. He has developed
great powers of mind, acquired much knowledge which he

can store in books, microfilms and computers. He can make powerful machines and generate great resources of energy. He has come of age intellectually and technologically, he has a mastery over things. Has his spiritual development kept pace?

PRAYERS

Human achievement

O Lord God, we thank thee that thy Spirit is ever urging the spirits of men to higher achievements of wisdom, skill, love and goodness. We praise thee for the developing universe, by obeying whose laws men can circle the earth and reach toward the stars. Grant thy wisdom and protection to those who would go still further, and help them to know that they can never overtake thee nor pass out of thy care, through thy perfect Son, Jesus Christ, our Lord.

Nuclear energy

O God of all wisdom and power, who art ever revealing thyself to those who seek for thee. Grant that men may not only discover the secrets of thy universe, but may use them according to thy will, not for destruction and war, but for the welfare of all thy people. We ask this in the name of Jesus Christ our Lord.

Answerable to God

O Father, I am your son, created by you; let me value my heredity and my heritage. O God, I am answerable to you; let me accept my responsibility to work with you to make the world of your will. O God, I depend on you; give me wisdom, inspiration and staying power. O Eternal One, my life in this world is limited; even now let me live in the dimension of eternity.

Blessed be thou, O God, who has shown me good and evil: enable me always to choose aright and to set my small will in the direction of thy good, loving, wise, all-embracing goodness.

7. A BEING ON THE WAY

It is instinctive in man to want to go beyond what men have already reached, whether in distance or achievement. His power over the world is ever growing. Yet the question must be asked as to whether man's inner nature is growing and deepening in a way commensurate with his control of nature outside himself. Is he happier, more integrated, less restless? Is he adventuring into the spiritual future, exploring the frontiers of the physical and the spiritual, life and death, time and eternity?

INSIGHTS FROM SCRIPTURE

Pressing on towards the goal
Not that I have already obtained this (i.e. the resurrection from the dead) or am already perfect; but I press on to make it my own, because Christ Jesus has made me his own.
Philippians 3: 12

Divine glory reflected
We all, with unveiled face, beholding the glory of the Lord, are being changed into his likeness from one degree of glory to another.
2 Corinthians 3: 18

Greater things ahead
Beloved, we are God's children now; it does not yet appear what we shall be, but we know that when he appears we shall be like him.
1 John 3: 2

The right milieu
If any one is in Christ, he is a new creation; the old has passed away, behold, the new has come.
2 Corinthians 5: 17

OTHER INSIGHTS

Divine burning

He will shake heaven and earth, that only the unshakeable may remain: he is a consuming fire, that only that which cannot be consumed may stand forth eternal. It is the nature of God, so terribly pure that it destroys all that is not pure as fire, which demands like purity in our worship. He will have purity. It is not that the fire will burn us if we do not worship thus; but that the fire will burn us until we worship thus; yea, will go on burning within us after all that is foreign to it has yielded to its force, no longer with pain and consuming, but as the highest consciousness of life, the presence of God.   *George Macdonald*

Nearing the goal

The centre of the soul is God, and when the soul has attained to him according to the whole capacity of its being, and according to the force of its operation, it will have reached the last and deep centre of the soul, which will be when with all its powers it loves and understands and enjoys God.   *St John of the Cross*

A Muslim prayer

I thank thee, Lord, for knowing me better than I know myself, and for letting me know myself better than others know me. Make me, I pray thee, better than they suppose, and forgive me for what they do not know.

Abu Bekr,
the father-in-law of Muhammad d. 634

PRAYERS

'Becoming' towards 'Being'

O Christ, you revealed the ultimate, the eternal, the divine in terms of human personality. Men are much the same today in the depths of their being as they were in the days of

your incarnation. Let me study the records of your pattern
of living. Let me commune with your eternal, ever-present
Spirit, and be cleansed, deepened, filled with love, moving
on to the fullness of being which is your will and in company
with my fellow disciples, O Christ, my Lord.

Not for ourselves

O Lord, we know that we are incompetent to heal ourselves, to sanctify ourselves, to transfigure ourselves. Our
holiness is your action in us, through our willingness to
accept the indwelling of your Spirit. Heal me, Lord. Sanctify me, Lord. Transfigure me, Lord. Fill me, Lord. Direct
me, Lord. Use me, Lord.

Blessed be thou, O Lord, for making me thy disciple and
leading me on to the perfection of being and blessing.

II. WHAT OF MY LIFE?

As I look at my life what can I learn from it? What understanding and inspiration can I find to live life well?

8. EXPERIENCE

People today are not prepared to take their faith from the tradition in which they were born, nor from other people. They want to deduce it from their own experience of life. They do not need theories, but the experience which will be the source of their own interpretation. They are suspicious of anything which seems to escape from life into theory, from experience into doctrine, or from the thing itself into talk about it. The method they want to follow is the inductive one rather than the deductive.

INSIGHTS FROM SCRIPTURE

O taste and see that the Lord is good!   *Psalm 34 : 8*

How sweet are thy words to my taste, sweeter than honey to my mouth!   *Psalm 119 : 103*

'Rabbi, where are you staying?' He said to them, 'Come and see.'   *John 1 : 38*

Those . . . who have tasted the heavenly gift, and have become partakers of the Holy Spirit, and have tasted the goodness of the word of God and the powers of the age to come.   *Hebrews 6 : 4*

OTHER INSIGHTS

Too few people have experienced the divine image as the innermost possession of their own souls. Christ only meets them from without, never from within the soul.   *C. G. Jung*

> Though Christ a thousand times
> In Bethlehem be born,
> If he's not born in thee
> Thy soul is still forlorn.

> The cross on Golgotha
> Will never save thy soul,
> The cross in thine own heart
> Alone can make thee whole.
>
> *Angelus Silesius*

People need to discover their own self-identity. Many go to
drugs, not to forget the miseries of life, but to discover its
secrets, to explore an inner life of identity, liberation and
happiness. The mystics tell us that this experience can be
gained from the discipline of meditation, entering into
silence, stilling the activity of the mind, allowing feelings and
intuitions to rise from the depths of our being.

PRAYERS

Fontal being
Give me a candle of the Spirit, O God, as I go down into the
deep of my own being. Show me the hidden things. Take me
down to the spring of my life, and tell me my nature and
name. Give me freedom to grow so that I may become the
self, the seed of which thou didst plant in me at my making.
Out of the deep I cry unto thee, O Lord.

Under thy hands
Grant, O my God, that I may keep myself under your
loving hands, so that you may complete the work begun in
me, and make me more holy, more humble, more loving,
more dependent on you, and more serviceable to you,
through Jesus Christ, my Saviour.

Experience of renewal
[We need to take time to experience the peace and re-
creating grace of God within our inmost being: to relax
all tension of the body, to quieten the thoughts of the mind,
and in the stillness let the peace of God flow into us, so that
we experience the divine peace as well as think about it. At
times when we are tired and under stress, it will; if we are

quiet and open, our Lord will fulfil his promise to refresh and renew us.]

Blessed be thou, O Lord, for thy creative hand upon me, for the experience of thy presence with me, thy strengthening, thy guiding, thy blessing.

9. ENJOYMENT OF THE WORLD

Given reasonable health and freedom from anxiety, the world is for most people a good place to live in, with much of interest, beauty and wonder. Contact with other people can bring friendship, co-operation, humour and enjoyment. Given the faith that the world is God's creation and that each man is made in the image of God in a unique and personal way, our enjoyment becomes increasingly right and satisfying. Add to this the availability of divine grace for every difficulty and opportunity, and our enjoyment becomes almost mandatory.

INSIGHTS FROM SCRIPTURE

The divine intention
And God saw everything that he had made, and behold, it was very good.   *Genesis 1:31*

Everything in Christ
For all things are yours, whether Paul or Apollos or Cephas or the world or life or death or the present or the future, all are yours; and you are Christ's; and Christ is God's.
                                              1 Corinthians 3:21–23

Everything for man
The sabbath was made for man, not man for the sabbath.
                                              Mark 2:27

He who did not spare his own Son, but gave him up for us all, will he not also give us all things with him?

Romans 8 : 32

OTHER INSIGHTS

Joy in created things

You never enjoy the world aright, till the Sea itself floweth in your veins, till you are clothed with the heavens, and crowned with the stars: and perceive yourself to be the sole heir of the whole world, and more than so, because men are in it who are every one sole heirs as well as you. Till you can sing and rejoice and delight in God, as misers do in gold, and Kings in sceptres, you never enjoy the world . . .

All things were made to be yours, and you were made to prize them according to their value: which is your office and duty, the end for which you were created, and the means whereby you enjoy. The end for which you were created, is that by prizing all that God hath done, you may enjoy yourself and him in Blessedness.   *Thomas Traherne*

Joy in created beings

> I did not think, I did not strive,
> The deep peace burnt my me alive;
> The bolted door had broken in,
> I knew that I had done with sin.
> I knew that Christ had given me birth
> To brother all the souls on earth,
> And every bird and every beast
> Should share the crumbs broke at the feast.

John Masefield
'The Everlasting Mercy'

Joy in Christ

We can trust him wholly with his world. We can trust him with ourselves. We are sure that he cares far more to make the best of us and to do the most through us, than we have ever cared ourselves. He is ever trying to make us under-

stand that he yearns to be to us more than aught in the universe besides. That he really wants us, and needs us, is the wonder and strength of our lives.　　　*A. W. Robinson*
'Personal life of the clergy'

PRAYERS

The author of beauty

Grant, O Lord, we pray thee, that as we look upon the beauty of the world, our hearts may be lifted to thee, who art more lovely than the things thou hast created, the first author of all beauty, who has prepared for them that love thee the vision of thy eternal loveliness, through Jesus Christ our Lord.　　　　　　　　　　　　　　　　　　Amen

The joy ahead

O God, who hast prepared for them that love thee such good things as pass man's understanding: Pour into our hearts such love toward thee, that we, loving thee above all things, may obtain thy promises, which exceed all that we can desire: through Jesus Christ our Lord. Amen.
Book of Common Prayer

All to enjoy

O God of all beauty, whose will it is that all thy creatures enjoy the world and the life thou hast given us; we know that many are unable to do this, through hunger, poverty, disease, oppression, ignorance, or sin. Let me never rest content in thy joys until I have done everything in my power and in thy grace to help others to share them also, O God of all goodness and willer of abundant life.

GLORIA

O the depths of the riches and wisdom and knowledge of God!... For from him and through him and to him are all things. To him be glory for ever. Amen. *Romans 11: 33, 36*

10. SLEEP

Sleep is necessary to renew the body's strength, and to rest and refresh the mind. Most of us spend one-third of each day in sleep. For the time being we consciously forget our activities, our problems, our fears, our hopes and plans, though sometimes these are so present and vivid that we get little sleep. When we sleep, what happens during this daily period of unconsciousness? Is not the sub-conscious mind still active and the spirit at the centre of our being sending us cleverly disguised messages through dreams, telling us things we need to know, informing us of fears, hopes, unfulfilled wishes operating in the depths?

INSIGHTS FROM SCRIPTURE

To sleep is to trust
And behold, there arose a great storm on the sea, so that the boat was being swamped by the waves; but he was asleep.
Matthew 8 : 24

Wisdom in sleep
It is in vain that ye rise up early and so late take rest, and eat the bread of toil; for so he giveth unto his beloved in sleep.
Psalm 127 : 2 (RV margin)

A watching presence
Behold, he who keeps Israel will neither slumber nor sleep.
Psalm 121 : 4

Then Jacob awoke from his sleep and said, 'Surely the Lord is in this place; and I did not know it.'
Genesis 28 : 16

OTHER INSIGHTS

As thy day
In the night of weariness let me give myself up to sleep without struggle, resting my trust upon thee. Let me not force my flagging spirit into a poor preparation for thy worship. It is thou who drawest the veil of night upon the tired eyes of the day to renew its sight in a fresher gladness of awakening.   *Rabindranath Tagore*

A theory of sleep
It may be said of the body in regard of sleep as well as in regard of death, 'It is sown in weakness, it is raised in power . . .' No one can deny the power of the wearied body to paralyse the soul; but I have a correlate theory which I love, and which I expect to find true – that, while the body wearies the mind, it is the mind that restores vigour of the body, and then, like the man who has built him a stately palace, rejoices to dwell in it. I believe that, if there be a living, conscious love at the heart of the universe, the mind, in the quiescence of its consciousness in sleep, comes into a less disturbed contact with its origin, the heart of the creation; whence gifted with calmness and strength for itself, it grows able to impart comfort and restoration to the weary frame. The cessation of labour affords but the necessary occasion; makes it possible, as it were, for the occupant of an outlying station in the wilderness to return to his Father's house for fresh supplies . . . The child-soul goes home at night, and returns in the morning to the labours of the school.   *George Macdonald*

PRAYERS

Leave it quietly to God
O God, you yourself never nod or sleep, but in your wisdom and mercy have given us the gift of sleep. Help me, tonight and every night, to leave my business in your hands, without

worry. Let me leave my loved ones and my suffering ones in your safe care. Let me relax and be my real self, taking off my poses with my clothes. Then you can speak to me in the depths of my being and dreams can bring me comfort and wisdom, O Creator of man and Giver of sleep.

Sleep
O God who hast given me such a wonderful nature, that even when I sleep my mind continues to think, giving me understanding of myself and clues how to live: help me to know my inner self and to trust it, for it is there that thy Spirit works. I praise thee, my God and Maker, who dost give gifts to thy loved ones, even while we sleep.

Dreams
O God, who through thy ordering of our inner nature dost show us truths about ourselves as we sleep: help us to interpret these messages from the depths of our being, and to know and accept ourselves as the starting-point for growth towards the pattern of thy Son, Jesus Christ our Lord.

In peace I will both lie down and sleep; for thou alone, O Lord, makest me dwell in safety.   *Psalm 4:8*

11. SUCCESS AND FAILURE

At times in the past, religious men have felt that if they are faithful to God, he must grant them success, guaranteeing them against defeat, suffering, failure. Men in misfortune sometimes ask 'What have I done that God should do this to me?' The answer is probably 'nothing', with the denial that God is responsible at all for the unfortunate happening, though there is still the mystery of his providence and the interlocking of cause and effect in the human scene. God promises that his grace shall be more than sufficient for every happening and that he will always be at work to

bring a greater blessing than if the unfortunate thing had
never happened.

INSIGHTS FROM SCRIPTURE

Every moment right
I have learned, in whatever state I am, to be content.
Philippians 4 : 11

God works for good, if . . .
We know that in everything God works for good with those
who love him, who are called according to his purpose.
Romans 8 : 28

Faith must not fail
Simon, Simon, behold, Satan demanded to have you, that
he might sift you like wheat, but I have prayed for you that
your faith may not fail.   *Luke 22 : 31–32*

Restoration after failure
'Simon, son of John, do you love me ?' . . . 'Lord, you know
everything; you know that I love you.' . . . 'Feed my
sheep.'   *John 21 : 17*

OTHER INSIGHTS

Reasons for failure
When we fail in our discipleship it is always for one of two
reasons; either we are not trying to be loyal, or else we are
trying in our own strength and find that is not enough. And
the better we are at our job, the greater our natural abilities,
the more subtle the temptation.   *William Temple*

The final chapter
At any point in his life a man may write under his own life
story so far the words 'To be continued'. The final chapter
always remains to be written, and it can be written in
co-authorship with God, if the man so wills. In the same way

God will write the final chapter in human history. A man's character determines and is determined by his response to external circumstances over which he has no control. Similarly the character of a nation and the rise and fall of a civilization.

All in God's hands
Nothing in the hands of God is evil; not failure, not thwarting, not the frustration of every hope or ambition, not death itself. All in his hands is success, and will bear the more fruit the more we leave it to him, having no ambitions, no preoccupations, no excessive preferences or desires of our own.
Archbishop Goodier

Freedom within
We are undefeated as long as we keep on trying, as long as we have some source of movement within ourselves and are not just moved by outside forces, as long as we retain the freedom of right decision and action, whatever the circumstances.

PRAYERS

Faithfulness and priority
O Lord our God, in whose hands is the issue of all things, who requirest from thy stewards not success, but faithfulness: give us such faith in thee, and in thy sure purpose that we measure not our lives by what we have done, or failed to do, but by our obedience to thy will.   *Daily Prayer*

To the very end
O Lord God, when thou givest to thy servants to endeavour any great matter, grant us also to know that it is not the beginning, but the continuing of the same unto the end, until it be thoroughly finished, which yieldeth the true glory; through him who for the finishing of thy work laid down his life, our redeemer, Jesus Christ.   *Francis Drake*

Thy will only

Dear Lord, quieten my spirit and fix my thoughts on thy will, that I may see what thou wouldest have done, and contemplate its doing without self-consciousness or inner excitement, without haste and without delay, without fear of other people's judgements or anxiety about success, knowing only that it is thy will and must therefore be done quietly, faithfully, and lovingly, for in thy will alone is our peace.

Blessed be thou, O my Lord, who dost not ask from me success, but only faithfulness to thy wise and loving will.

12. OLD AGE

Many people as they grow older fear the coming of old age. They regret the failing of physical and mental powers, the withdrawal from active life, posts of leadership and the satisfaction of being used creatively. These increasing diminishments can be seen as a hollowing-out of the material and the temporal, in order to be ready to be filled with the spiritual and the eternal.

INSIGHTS FROM SCRIPTURE

A divine responsibility

Even to your old age I am He, and to grey hairs I will carry you. I have made, and I will bear.   *Isaiah 46:4*

Still creative

They still bring forth fruit in old age, they are ever full of sap and green.   *Psalm 92:14*

Growing in wisdom

So teach us to number our days that we may get a heart of wisdom.   *Psalm 90:12*

Living in the present
He will not much remember the days of his life because God
keeps him occupied with joy in his heart.

Ecclesiastes 5 : 20

At every stage
You have kept the good wine until now.　　　*John 2 : 10*

OTHER INSIGHTS

The real sources of strength
Gentlemen, when a man grows older and sees more deeply
into life, he does not find, if he possesses any inner world at
all, that he is advanced by the external march of things, by
the 'progress of civilization'. Nay, he feels himself, rather,
where he was before, and forced to seek the sources of
strength which his forefathers also sought. He is forced to
make himself a native of the Kingdom of God, the Kingdom
of the Eternal, the Kingdom of Love; and he comes to
understand that it was only of the Kingdom that Jesus Christ
desired to testify, and he is grateful to him for it.

Professor Harnack

When the signs of age begin to mark my body (and still
more when they touch my mind); when the ill that is to
diminish me or carry me off strikes from without or is born
within me; when the painful moment comes in which I
suddenly awaken to the fact that I am ill or growing old;
and above all at that last moment when I feel I am losing
hold of myself and am absolutely passive within the hands
of the great unknown forces that have formed me; in all
those dark moments, O God, grant that I may understand
that it is You (provided only my faith is strong enough) who
are painfully parting the fibres of my being in order to
penetrate to the very marrow of my substance and bear me
away within Yourself.　　　*Teilhard de Chardin*

Explorers

Old people are approaching a new frontier. Some will have a quiet faith in the God and Father of Jesus and will live each day as it comes, taking the crossing into the new dimension in their stride. Others will want to explore, experiencing the spiritual dimension within their own being, learning from those who left insights before they crossed, living now in the values of the beyond, recognizing that the only currency they can take with them is love.

PRAYERS

I have scaled the peak, and found no shelter in fame's bleak and barren height. Lead me, my Guide, before the light fades, into the valley of quiet where life's harvest mellows into golden wisdom.   *Rabindranath Tagore*

Grant, O Lord, that the years that are left may be the holiest, the most loving, the most mature. I thank you for the past and especially that you have kept the good wine until now. Help me to accept diminishing powers as the opportunity to prepare my soul for the full and free life to come in the state prepared by your Son, Jesus Christ, our Lord.

O God my Creator, O Jesus Christ my Teacher and Guide, O Holy Spirit my constant Companion, I thank you for my life and all who have loved, encouraged and inspired me. I would be more with you as I prepare for my last birth. I gratefully accept the forgiveness you offer as I look back from the border of my new country to the stretches of my first and much loved country. I hope, O Guardian of my soul, to be welcomed by the loved ones gone ahead, and not to lose touch with the loved ones I shall one day leave. I believe, O Creator and Saviour, that there is more love, more life ahead in the eternal home of the spirits of us all, which you have prepared in your undying love.

Blessed be God for my birth, my life and all the love I have enjoyed. Now, as always, I am in thy hands and nothing can take me away. And more blessing to come, Blessed Lord.

13. STANDING UP TO LIFE

Sooner or later suffering, misfortune, trouble come to every life. Some of it comes from our own ignorance, some from our own mistakes, some is a consequence of our own sin. But in almost every life there is a residue which seems inexplicable. Our Christian faith does not completely explain the mystery of suffering. It teaches us how to deal with suffering. It assures us that God does not will suffering, but he is in it, to redeem it and to turn it into good and blessing. Let us also remember that the perfect life was not exempt from suffering.

INSIGHTS FROM SCRIPTURE

Nothing shall defeat us
In all these things (trouble, danger, war, hunger, life, death) . . . we are more than conquerors through him who loved us.   *Romans 8 : 37*

No permanent harm
When you pass through the waters I will be with you; and through the rivers, they shall not overwhelm you; when you walk through fire you shall not be burned, and the flame shall not consume you.   *Isaiah 43 : 2*

Never defeated
We may be knocked down but we are never knocked out! . . . always 'going through it' yet never 'going under'.
                                        2 Corinthians 4 : 9, 6 : 9
                                                (Phillips)

In God's eternal Kingdom

He will wipe away every tear from their eyes, and death shall be no more, neither shall there be mourning nor crying nor pain any more, for the former things have passed away.

Revelation 21 : 4

OTHER INSIGHTS

How to react

When trouble hits us we can react to it in a variety of ways. We can let it knock us out, so that we lose all hope and stamina. We can rebel and refuse to accept the rightness or merit of it. We can fill our lives with feverish activity so that we have no time to think about it. Or we can accept it – without defeat, rebellion or evasion – trusting that God will make clear tomorrow what is so difficult to understand today.

Making a friend of pain

Holding the rebel post since set of sun,
Against those odds he knew resistance vain,
Yet fought all night, that fierce and foolish one,
Not till the morning's bugles blew a last
'Cease fire' he bowed his ravaged head, and cast
Weapons aside; climbed down the shattered stair,
Unbarred his door and made a friend of pain.

Punch

Providence?

'We mustn't question the ways of Providence,' said the Rector. 'Providence?' said the old woman. 'Don't you talk to me about Providence. I've had enough of Providence. First he took my husband, and then he took my 'taters, but there's one above as'll teach him to mind his manners, if he doesn't look out!' The Rector was too much distressed to challenge this remarkable piece of theology.

Dorothy Sayers
'The Nine Tailors'

Undefeated

He said not: Thou shalt not be tempested, thou shalt not be travailed, thou shalt not be afflicted; but he said: Thou shalt not be overcome.   *Mother Julian of Norwich*

PRAYERS

Holding on

O God, I bring this situation to thee and hold it to thee, refusing to let it get away from thee, believing that by thy grace, in answer to my prayer it will change, that something will turn up that was not there before, that the mountain of difficulty will be removed or thy wisdom show me the way to go round or thy grace strengthen me to climb over it or tunnel through it. Let me hold on in faith and love, O Lord my God.

Strengthen my back

Lord, teach me the art of patience while I am well, and give me the use of it when I am sick. In that day either lighten my burden or strengthen my back. Make me, who so often in my health have discovered my weakness, presuming on my own strength, to be strong in my sickness when I solely rely on thy assistance. Through Jesus Christ my Lord.
                                                    Thomas Fuller

Never doubting

Merciful God, be thou now unto us a strong tower of defence. Give us grace to await thy leisure, and patiently to bear what thou doest unto us, nothing doubting thy goodness towards us. Therefore do with us in all things as thou wilt: only arm us, we beseech thee, with thy armour, that we may stand fast; above all things taking to us the shield of faith, praying always that we may refer ourselves wholly to thy will, being assuredly persuaded that all thou doest cannot but be well. And unto thee be all honour and glory.   *Lady Jane Grey*

Grant, O Lord, that in everything that happens, I may see you drawing near, and hear you saying 'It is I. Be not afraid.'

14. DEATH AND BEYOND

Death is part of the future for everyone. It is the last post of this life and the reveillé of the next. Everywhere men fear death – it is the end of our present life, it is parting from loved ones, it is setting out into the unknown. We overcome death by accepting it as the will of a loving God; by finding him in it. Death, like birth, is only a transformation, another birth. When I die I shall change my state, that is all. And in faith in God, it is as easy and natural as going to sleep here and waking up there.

INSIGHTS FROM SCRIPTURE

Release from fear
He himself likewise partook of the same nature, that through death he might destroy him who has the power of death . . . and deliver all those who through fear of death were subject to lifelong bondage. *Hebrews 2 : 14–15*

Either way
If we live, we live to the Lord, and if we die, we die to the Lord; so then, whether we live or whether we die, we are the Lord's. For to this end Christ died and lived again, that he might be Lord both of the dead and of the living.
Romans 14 : 8–9

The source of deathless life
I am the resurrection and the life; he who believes in me, though he die, yet shall he live, and whoever lives and believes in me shall never die. *John 11 : 25–26*

A gem from the Jewish Torah
The eternal God is your dwelling place, and underneath
are the everlasting arms. *Deuteronomy 33 : 27*

OTHER INSIGHTS

Going home

> I have seen death too often to believe in death.
> It is not an ending – but a withdrawal.
> As one who finishes a long journey,
>> Stills the motor,
>> Turns off the lights,
>> Steps from his car,
> And walks up the path
> To the home that awaits him. *Blanding*

Death as a guest
On the day when death will knock at thy door what wilt
thou offer to him? Oh, I will set before my guest the full
vessel of my life – I will never let him go with empty hands.
All the sweet vintage of all my autumn days and summer
nights, all the earnings and gleanings of my busy life will I
place before him at the close of my days when death will
knock at my door. *Rabindranath Tagore*

Need to be emptied
God must, in some way or other, make room for Himself,
hollowing us out and emptying us, if He is finally to
penetrate into us. And in order to assimilate us in Him, He
must break the molecules of our being so as to re-cast and
re-model us. The function of death is to provide the necessary entrance into our inmost selves. It will make us undergo
the required dissociation. It will put us into the state
organically needed if the divine fire is to descend upon us.
And in that way its fatal power to decompose and dissolve
will be harnessed to the most sublime operations of life.
Teilhard de Chardin

Parting Greeting
Not an end but a beginning, not a death but a new birth,
not 'farewell', but 'happy birthday'.

PRAYERS

Within call
O Christ, the little girl on her deathbed, the young man on
the way to his grave, and Lazarus three days in the tomb,
could all hear your voice. May each soul as it passes through
death, hear your friendly voice, see the look of love in your
eyes and the smile of welcome in your face, and be led by
you to the Father of all souls.

Still united
O Lord our God, from whom neither life nor death can
separate those who trust in thy love, and whose love holds
in its embrace thy children in this world and the next;
so unite us to thyself that in fellowship with thee we may
always be united to our loved ones whether here or there:
give us courage, constancy and hope; through him who
died and was buried and rose again for us, Jesus Christ our
Lord.   *William Temple*

A clearer light
O Lord God, thou knowest how much the souls of the
departed need thy cleansing and forgiveness, before they
are ready to be at home in thy presence. Grant that in the
clearer light of Paradise they may see their need and accept
the grace thou hast been offering them since the moment of
their creation. So, most gracious God, thou wilt be their
Redeemer as well as their Creator, and all through Jesus
Christ, our Lord.

Into thy hands
Lord, as my mortal hours run by, help me to die to the

flesh, die to myself, die to all that is not of thy Spirit, die daily. So that I make the last surrender of this life, not to death, but to God.

Give my soul hunger for its re-making by its Beloved, in light: and bring me to the finishing of faith, to my own Easter Day, IN THEE. *Eric Milner-White*

III. WITH WHOM?

*How are we to think of others,
feel about them, act towards them?*

15. A ROYAL LAW

The second great commandment of the Law of the Lord was a miracle of inspiration, combining divine inspiration and human perception. To love my neighbour as myself, to give him equal value and equal rights, to do nothing to him which I would not want done to myself, and more positively to do to him only those deeds that I would like done to me, is a principle that makes for a human and satisfying society, and it makes for a heart at peace and moving out in love.

INSIGHTS FROM SCRIPTURE

God-given
It is not good that the man should be alone.
Genesis 2:18

The reason why
You shall love your neighbour as yourself: I am the Lord.
Leviticus 19:18

A law of the Kingdom
If you really fulfil the royal law . . . 'You shall love your neighbour as yourself,' you do well.
James 2:8

Where will it end?
And who is my neighbour?
Luke 10:29

Judging another?
It is before his own master that he stands or falls.
Romans 14:4

OTHER INSIGHTS

I am always neighbour
Most of us want the appearance of honouring this imperative

to love our neighbour, but try to limit its application, as the
legalistic questioner implied in his question, which drew
from Jesus the immortal parable of the Good Samaritan.
To the question 'And who is my neighbour?', the reply of
Jesus is in effect 'Stop asking this question! *You* are always
the neighbour. Go and do as the Samaritan did.'

The neighbour spirit

True neighbourliness must begin within our own psychological attitudes. I must accept my neighbour for what he
is, I must let him be himself, respect his 'isness' and self-
understanding. I must not impose my pattern on him or
exploit him for my own purposes. I must be interested in
him as a person, so that our relationship will encourage
mutual development in maturity. Further, I must be ready
to take initiatives, to engage in adventures of understanding and friendship.

How to begin

We learned to love by being loved. The apostle of love tells
us that we love God because he first loved us. In the same
way, as little children we learned to love by experiencing
the love of our parents and those in the family circle of love.
Having experienced love, and having responded to love, we
let the love received and returned move outwards in ever
widening circles.

PRAYERS

My neighbour

O God, I thank thee for my fellow-man without whom I
would have no personal relationship, and on whose work I
depend for the continuation of my life. Let me always
respect him, never try to exploit him, always be open to
him, never presume to classify him, but always be reverent
to his mystery and selfhood. Let my heart go out to greet
him, let the smile in my eyes welcome him, in desire for true
relationship, O Father of us both.

Let them come
O Creator Lord, let me feel the 'isness' of things and people, without resistance, without trying to impose my own pattern upon them or exploit them for selfish ends. Let me welcome them, enjoy them, value them, love them, for what they are and for what they are becoming through your creative love.

A radiation exercise
[Beginning from within the heart, and sending out to those near to us, then in widening circles to others in our village or town, to those of our own nation, then neighbouring nations, 'till finally the whole of mankind, living and departed, is reached in the radiation in turn of goodwill, compassion, love, joy, peace, blessing, remembering that these lovely dispositions start from God within ourselves and are reinforced by his infinitely more generous radiation.]

Blessed be thou, O God – my Father, his Father, her Father, their Father, our Father.

16. PEOPLE IN NEED

Nowadays we know much more about the world than people of previous generations. The news media bring us immediate reports of emergencies and catastrophes. It is not just a matter of helping an occasional neighbour in need, but the billions of people who do not get enough food to eat, who are in the grip of poverty and disease. Our hearts fail when we think that half the people in the world are under-nourished, and there are more homeless, stateless people than in any earlier generation. We can be grateful that the nations of the world are learning Christ's compassion and are co-operating in the United Nations Food and Agriculture Organization, the World Health Organization, the relief of refugees, the care of handicapped children. The duty of neighbour now extends to nations as well as to individuals.

INSIGHTS FROM SCRIPTURE

The divine intention
They shall hunger no more, neither thirst any more . . . (God) shall wipe away every tear from their eyes, and death shall be no more, neither shall there be mourning nor crying nor pain any more, for the former things have passed away.
Revelation 7:16, 21:4

Then he showed me the river of the water of life . . . on either side of the river, the tree of life with its twelve kinds of fruit, yielding its fruit each month; and the leaves of the tree were for the healing of the nations.   *Revelation 22:1–2*

Nations will be judged
Before him will be gathered all the nations . . . and he will say to them 'Truly, I say to you, as you did it not to one of the least of these, you did it not to me.'
Matthew 25:32,45

Share what you have
Now the day began to wear away; and the twelve came and said to him, 'Send the crowd away, to go into the villages and country round about, to lodge and get provisions' . . . But he said to them, 'You give them something to eat.'
Luke 9:12–13

OTHER INSIGHTS

Hungry men have no ears
The millions of hungry men in the world have no ears for reason. They have only stomachs. Those who fill them will earn their life-long gratitude and allegiance – whatever their way of life. On our ability to grow sufficient, cheap food,

depends not only our way of life, but also the future of humanity. *Max Warren*

Ridding our hearts of selfishness
He would have urged all Christians to fulfil their duties in a world that still belongs to God despite its sin and shame. But equally firmly he would have declared that no scheme for social betterment, no international organization, no political or ecclesiastical reform can in themselves heal the wounds of humanity. In one way only can men be saved, by ridding their hearts of the selfishness which hides from them the knowledge of the love of God. Once that love can gain admittance, lighting up the whole universe as the sun breaks through the clouds at the end of a day of sodden rain, then the whole quality of life is changed and inevitably men will go out to help their fellow-men. *Florence Higham*
'Frederick Denison Maurice'

'As cold as charity'
There is a danger in our modern world that charity has become so organized and impersonal that the spirit of warm humble service gets forgotten. Only a sense of personal concern and ministering love can heal and hearten.

PRAYERS

Need or greed
O Lord, we know that we live in a world of plenty, with food sufficient for all. Help us to realize that there is enough for everyone's need, but not enough for everyone's greed. Give us hearts of compassion, unselfish concern and loving care, that all may have the abundant life which is thy will. When we offer all that we have, we know that in thy hands there is enough and to spare, O Lord of the hungry crowd and of the twelve basketsful left over.

For social justice
O, Lord, we pray thee that thou wilt hasten the time when

no man shall live in contentment while he knows that others have need. Inspire in us and in men of all nations the desire for social justice, that the hungry may be fed, the homeless welcomed, the sick healed, and a just and peaceful order established in the world, according to thy gracious will made known in Jesus Christ, our Lord.

For homecoming
O Christ our Lord, who didst go forth in homelessness that thou mightest find a home in every man, and that every man might find a home in thee. We bring before thee at this time all thy homeless ones, all who are in exile or in suffering. Grant them the sense of being held fast in thee, and enable all who love thee to strive together for a world which shall be closer to thy Kingdom in which men may live together as a family, each caring for all, and all caring for each, for the sake of peace.

To thee, O Creator of the seed and of the fertility of the soil and the thirty-fold harvest, be praise and glory from all thy creatures.

17. ENEMIES

Enemies are more our neighbours than we think for they occupy a good deal of our attention and stir up a good deal of our emotion. Common sense would urge us to deal with this relationship. Religion is even more emphatic, and Jesus taught us that the love which we receive from God must know no boundaries. It must reach out to embrace everyone, including those whom we regard as enemies, and those who regard us as such.

INSIGHTS FROM SCRIPTURE

The divine example
You have heard that it was said, 'You shall love your neighbour and hate your enemy.' But I say to you, Love

your enemies and pray for those who persecute you, so that
you may be sons of your Father who is in heaven.

Matthew 5 : 43–45

The only cure
Hatred ceases not by hatred, but by love.   *The Buddha*

Putting it into practice
Father, forgive them; for they know not what they do.

Luke 23 : 34

A faithful follower
(Stephen) knelt down and cried with a loud voice, 'Lord,
do not hold this sin against them.'   *Acts 7 : 60*

OTHER INSIGHTS

A Muslim example
When he was brought to be crucified and saw the cross and
the nails, he turned to the people and uttered a prayer,
ending with the words, 'And these thy servants who are
gathered to slay me, in zeal for thy religion and in desire to
win thy favour, forgive them, O Lord, and have mercy
upon them; for verily if thou hadst revealed to them that
which thou hast revealed to me, they would not have done
what they have done; and if thou hadst hidden from me
that which thou hast hidden from them, I should not have
suffered this tribulation. Glory unto thee in whatsoever thou
doest, and glory unto thee in whatsoever thou willest.'

Al Hallaj
(Crucified 922)

An Elizabethan prayer
Let not their first hating of us turn to their harm, seeing
that we cannot do them good for want of ability. Lord, we
desire their amendment and our own. Separate them not
from us by punishing them, but join them and knit them to
us by thy favourable dealing with them.

J.S.   C

What prayer accomplishes
Prayer for one who counts himself an enemy or whom I
have labelled an enemy, ends his isolation. He is now
included within the circle of loving concern. His isolation or
his expulsion or his withdrawal is ended.

PRAYERS

The prayer of St Francis
> Lord, make us instruments of thy peace,
> > Where there is hatred, let us sow love;
> > Where there is injury, pardon;
> > Where there is discord, union;
> > Where there is doubt, faith;
> > Where there is despair, hope;
> > Where there is darkness, light;
> > Where there is sadness, joy;
> For thy mercy and thy truth's sake. Amen

A disarming exercise
[Let me hold quietly in my mind before God the names of
people whom I find difficult, who have been critical of me,
of whom I am apprehensive or jealous or envious, any who
may have done me a bad turn, all whom I find it difficult to
love, praying that his goodwill may be done for them as for
myself. We are both then within the circle of God's forgiveness and love.]

Coals of fire
Lord, it is not easy to love unfriendly people with loving
warmth, but I would wish them well. Lord, I know that
heaping coals of fire on their head is not a respectable way
of getting my own back. I do not know its meaning, but it
must be something generous and good for you commanded
it, and I am your follower.

Lord Jesus Christ, thou art their Saviour and mine; draw
us closer to thee so that we come closer to one another.

18. WORLD CITIZENS

The world is rapidly becoming one through ease and speed of travel, through radio which brings us news and views in a fraction of a second, through the interdependence of nations, through the organization of ever greater units of association, through the United Nations Organization and its agencies. It is as if pressure from within the world process and the organization of mankind is pressing us towards human unity. The whole world is now one great neighbourhood. The idea of neighbour has expanded to embrace the whole of mankind in one universal citizenship which demands implementation.

INSIGHTS FROM SCRIPTURE

A universal covenant
This is the sign of the covenant which I make between me and you and every living creature that is with you, for all future generations: I set my bow in the cloud, and it shall be a sign of the covenant between me . . . and every living creature of all flesh.
Genesis 9 : 12–15

A universal blessing
I will make of you a great nation, and I will bless you, and make your name great, so that you will be a blessing . . . and by you all the families of the earth shall bless themselves.
Genesis 12 : 2–3

An eternal plan
For he has made known to us the mystery of his will, according to his purpose which he set forth in Christ as a plan for the fullness of time, to unite all things in him, things in heaven and things on earth.
Ephesians 1 : 9–10

All God's people
In that day Israel will be the third with Egypt and Assyria, a blessing in the midst of the earth, whom the Lord of hosts has blessed, saying, 'Blessed be Egypt my people, and Assyria the work of my hands, and Israel my heritage.'

Isaiah 19 : 24–25

OTHER INSIGHTS

A vision of faith
St Paul sees in Jesus the coming of a new man, man as God meant him to be. Jesus is not just one lonely individual but the beginning of a new creation, the spearhead of a new humanity. By our participation in the old humanity we share its mortality. Incorporated with Christ, we share his deathless life. More than this, Paul sees an eternal purpose, unperceived in past ages, to bring all things and all men into a unity in Christ.

An ineffective agent
The Church is meant to be the agent of salvation and unity for the whole world, but its disunity is holding up the unity of mankind. In many instances it is a divisive influence instead of a unifying one. We Christians need to pray and work for the unity of the Church according to Christ's will and in the way that he will show us.

A long way to go
With honesty and candour we must turn to the catalogue of human divisiveness, strife and mutual hostility as we consider this theme. The validity of the idea of a natural human unity inexorably finding its expression in history is simply not self-evident. The cheerful signs of increasing brotherhood and the imminent reunion of the family of man are pleasing to behold. But they must be scrutinized in company with their opposites, which are the signs of rampant disorder and deterioration of the human community.

J. Robert Nelson

PRAYERS

One blood

O God, who hast made of one blood all nations of the earth and didst send thy blessed Son to be the redeemer of all mankind, unite us in our common humanity and make us one new man in the same thy Son, Jesus Christ, our Lord.

The Ingathering

Look with love, O God, upon your family the whole human race, scattered throughout the earth. Gather us from all corners of the world to your presence, opened for us by your Son, Jesus Christ. We pray for all people who worship you under symbols received from their ancient traditions and through the experience of the Holy Spirit working in the depths of their hearts. Hasten the time when we shall all come to the fullness of truth and the enjoyment of your salvation, O God, Creator, Saviour and Sanctifier of all.

The long travail

Grant us to look with thine eyes of compassion, O merciful God, at the long travail of mankind – the wars, the hungry millions, the countless refugees, the natural disasters, the cruel and needless deaths, men's inhumanity to one another, the heartbreak and hopelessness of so many lives. Hasten the coming of the messianic age when the nations shall be at peace, and men shall live free from fear and free from want and there shall be no more pain or tears, in the security of thy will and the assurance of thy love, shown us in Jesus the Christ, the Saviour of all.

O Christ, thou art God's appointed leader in the eternal plan to gather everything and everyone into the divine love. Thou art my leader too – let me see thy footmarks always ahead and in them plant my own.

19. PEOPLE OF OTHER FAITHS

People of other faiths are our spiritual neighbours in the journey of life and in the search for spiritual dimensions and values. The outgoing Christian mission has made them neighbours and has stimulated them to examine their own religious traditions. The ease of travel and the development of trade brings them to our countries, so they are now physical as well as spiritual neighbours. Their presence makes them our neighbours, as well as their interest in religious questions. We have to interpret the second great commandment in our attitude towards them.

INSIGHTS FROM SCRIPTURE

Not only true within Judaism
Think not that I have come to abolish the law and the prophets; I have come not to abolish them but to fulfil them.
Matthew 5 : 17

A Gentile's faith commended
Truly I say to you, not even in Israel have I found such faith.
Matthew 8 : 10

On their hearts as well as on ours
When Gentiles who have not the law do by nature what the law requires, they are a law to themselves . . . They show that what the law requires is written on their hearts.
Romans 2 : 14–15

Not the only bearers of truth
'Teacher . . . we forbade him because he was not following us.' . . . 'Do not forbid him . . . For he that is not against us is for us.'
Mark 9 : 38–40

Faithfulness to received truth essential to more truth
If they do not hear Moses and the prophets, neither will
they be convinced if some one should rise from the dead.

Luke 16:31

OTHER INSIGHTS

Creator of all
If we believe in God as Creator we must surely think of him
as wanting to make an impact on all, through their history,
their experience, their prophets. We believe that he is the
source of all truth, goodness and love, so where we see signs
of these we must surely believe that he has been active.

A spirit of appreciation
We recognize as part of the truth that sense of the majesty
of God and the consequent reverence in worship which are
conspicuous in Islam; the deep sense of the world's sorrow
and unselfish search for the way of escape which are at the
heart of Buddhism; the desire for contact with ultimate
reality conceived as spiritual which is prominent in Hindu-
ism; the belief in a moral order in the universe and consequent insistence on moral conscience which are enun-
ciated by Confucianism; the disinterested pursuit of truth
and of human welfare which are often found in those who
stand for the secular civilization but do not accept Christ
as their Lord and Saviour.   *Jerusalem Conference* 1928

Only one divine light
From the beginning the divine light has shone. Always it was
coming into the world; always it enlightened every man
alive in his reason and conscience. Every check on animal
lust felt by the primitive savage, every stimulation to a nobler
life, is God self-revealed within his soul . . . So it may be truly
said that the conscience of the heathen man is the voice of
Christ within him – though muffled by his ignorance. All
that is noble in the non-Christian systems of thought, or
conduct, or worship is the work of Christ upon them and

within them. By the Word of God – that is to say, by Jesus Christ – Isaiah, and Plato, and Zoroaster, and Buddha, and Confucius conceived and uttered such truths as they declared. There is only one divine light; and every man in his measure is enlightened by it.   *William Temple*

PRAYERS

Seekers of truth

O eternal Word, who from the beginning hast revealed glimpses of truth and righteousness through prophets of many faiths; we praise thee that all that is of value is found fulfilled and perfected in thee, and all that is mistaken finds its correction in thee. Do thou draw all seekers of truth and righteousness to thyself, and vouchsafe to them the unsearchable riches that can be found in thee alone.

Personal encounter

O Spirit of God, guide me as I seek to discover thy working with men of other faiths. Give me the strength of truth, the gentleness and strength of love, the clear eye of judgement, and the courage of faith. Above all, grant me a deeper understanding of him who is the Truth, a greater commitment to him who is the Lord, a deeper gratitude to him who is the Saviour of all, even Jesus Christ thy Eternal Word, through whom thou art drawing all men to thyself, that they may be saved for ever, and worship thee the only true God, blessed for evermore.

Guidance for encounter

O Eternal Lord God, the Creator and Saviour of all men, I pray thee to guide me with thy Holy Spirit as I meet men of other faiths. Grant me friendliness to arouse their confidence, patience to listen, and wisdom to understand what they say; and readiness to learn any truth they have from thee, any ways of goodness by which they seek to live. Help me to speak without self-consciousness or self-assertion of my faith in thee and of what thou hast done for me. Guard me against all compromise with truth and give me the penetrating insight of thy Word, quick to discern the inmost thoughts of the heart. Save me from the presumption of defending thee who didst put thyself at the mercy of men at Bethlehem and Calvary. Invest me with thine own love for those I meet and give me a word to forward thy purpose for each. And ever purify my faith and worship, that I may become more wholly thine, through Jesus Christ, my Lord and Saviour, and the Lord and Saviour of all.

Blessed be thou, O Lord God, who hast not left thyself without witness in every age and in every generation.

20. OPEN HEARTS

People can sense when we are concerned and interested. Sometimes it may be that we are preoccupied with some problem or too much under the pressure of time, or it may be that we cannot take the trouble. We need to give our whole attention to our neighbour, to identify ourselves with him, to have an open ear, an open mind and an open heart. This applies not only to individual relationships, but also to the relationship of our social, national and religious groupings as we meet similar neighbour groups.

INSIGHTS FROM SCRIPTURE

A good invitation
Is your heart true to my heart as mine is to yours? . . . If it is, give me your hand.   *2 Kings 10 : 15*

Patient understanding
But the man of God said, 'Let her alone, for she is in bitter distress; and the Lord has hidden it from me, and has not told me.'   *2 Kings 4 : 27*

A good prayer
Give thy servant therefore an understanding mind.

1 Kings 3 : 9

A warm welcome
Welcome one another, therefore, as Christ has welcomed you, for the glory of God.

Romans 15 : 7

OTHER INSIGHTS

The divine example
We remember how patiently and lovingly Jesus dealt with the woman who had the chronic haemorrhage, who waylaid him on the way to meet the urgent need of Jairus and his wife. We can imagine the impatient urgency of Jairus at the delay. Jesus quietly and unhurriedly dealt with the woman's need and then went on quietly and confidently to recall the little girl to life.

Wide-open hearts
Perhaps few among you have so many dealings with men of different races, different religions, different beliefs and different cultures as I – unworthily – have. In all these dealings I have always found a great love, a wide-open heart, always opens the hearts of others. This great love must be not mere diplomacy but the result of a sincere conviction that, as I have already said, we are all the children of one God, who has created mankind, who has created each one of us, and whose children we all are.

Cardinal Bea

The soul of the faith
When throughout the centuries have Judaism and Christianity looked each other full in the face? When did they frankly, honestly converse – frankly, wishing and daring to speak of the soul of the faith, the very heart of the belief; honestly, with that sympathy which is essential to human understanding?

Rabbi Leo Baeck

PRAYERS

For open minds
Grant, O Lord God, that we may wait anxiously, as servants
standing in the presence of their lord, for the least hint of
thy will; that we may welcome all truth, under whatever
outward forms it be uttered; that we may have grace to
receive new thoughts with grace, recognizing that thy ways
are not as our ways nor thy thoughts as our thoughts; that
we may bless every good deed, by whomsoever it may be
done; that we may rise above all party strife and cries to the
contemplation of the eternal Truth and Goodness, O God
Almighty who never changest; through thy Son, our
Saviour Jesus Christ. Amen   *Charles Kingsley*

An understanding heart
Grant me, O Lord, an understanding heart, that I may see
into the hearts of thy people, and know their strengths and
weaknesses, their hopes and despairs, their efforts and
failures, their need of love and their need to love. Through
my touch with them grant comfort and hope, and the
assurance that new life begins at any age and on any day,
redeeming the past, sanctifying the present, and brightening
the future with the assurance of thy unfailing love, brought
to me in Jesus Christ, thy Son, my Lord.

Upward and outward
Lord, my thoughts turn in upon myself. Turn them upward
to thee and outward to thy other children, that I may forget
myself, and lose all fear and anxiety, all self-seeking and
self-consciousness, in worship of thee and in love of others.
O save me from myself to worship, love and serve in
perfect freedom.

Blessed art thou, my Lord, present with every man,
knocking at each man's door, working among every human
grouping, to forward thy truth and spread thy love.

21. CAN I BE OF ANY HELP?

People want most of all someone who will stand with them in sympathy and understanding, with continuing concern and interest. They do not want Job's comforters who think they can diagnose, judge, explain, prescribe.

I must be ready to say 'Yes' in some way to everyone who comes, not necessarily to do all that is asked, but to be positive in response, eager to help. With this attitude the possible way, the best way, the right way will become clear.

INSIGHTS FROM SCRIPTURE

Not for myself alone
The water that I shall give him will become in him a spring of water welling up to eternal life. *John 4:14*

Identification with others
Then I came to them of the captivity . . . and I sat where they sat. *Ezekiel 3:15* (AV)

No limit
There is nothing love cannot face.; there is no limit to its faith, its hope, and its endurance.
1 Corinthians 13:7 (NEB)

Enough
The sisters sent a message to him: 'Sir, you should know that your friend lies ill.' *John 11:3* (NEB)

Christ's law
Help one another to carry these heavy loads, and in this way you will fulfil the law of Christ. *Galatians 6:2* (NEB)

OTHER INSIGHTS

Two types
People can be divided into two – those who drain us of our vitality and those who make us feel more alive. In a reciprocal way, I have to ask if I have the overflowing vitality of which Jesus spoke, sufficient not only for my own needs, but an available surplus for others. If I have not, then it is clear that I have not drunk from the eternal spring.

Go via God
We can often help others best not by going immediately and directly to them, but by going first to God for them. With his infinite compassion and love added to ours, open to any inspiration that he may give us, as well as being sensitive to their feelings and deeper needs, we can help them better, even if it is difficult to say a comforting word or do a helpful thing.

People ought to be able to say
'These Christians behave rather differently from what we used to think. They are interested in the things that interest us. They care about them. They share them with us. They are good at them. They do not preach at us about our being wrong in our assumptions. But they begin to make us feel that we are wrong in our assumptions, by being the sort of people that they are. They share our work with us. They are always alongside us. They really do know, they really do care, but they bring to it something different, something different which makes us think.'   *Michael Ramsey*

PRAYERS

Equally dear to God
O God, grant that I may reverence my fellow-men as created by thee and destined for eternity with thee. Grant that in our contact with one another, each of us may be

encouraged to grow to that which is thy will, in the knowledge that we are equally and infinitely dear to thee, and that thou wilt never let us go, never let us down, and never let us off until we are recognizably brothers of thy unique and perfect Son, Jesus Christ, and of one another.

Grace to love

Give us grace, O God our Father, to keep this day and always the new commandment and the great commandment and all the commandments, by loving thee with all our mind and soul and strength, and one another for thy sake; in the name of Jesus Christ our Lord.　　*Eric Milner-White*

Bring each to God

O God, I bring to you . . . and . . . and . . . Do for them, O dear Father, according to their needs. You know them better than I do, you love them more than I do. Your plan for them is better than I can imagine; let your good will be done, O God of us all.

Far be it from me that I should sin against the Lord by ceasing to pray for you.　　　　　　*1 Samuel 12:23*

IV. HOW SHALL I LIVE?

What attitudes, what inner characteristics,
what discipline should guide me?

22. BECOME AS A CHILD

Sometimes a saying of Jesus speaks directly and immediately to heart and mind. It is so simple and profound that we find it difficult to express more simply and fully. Such a saying is that about the need to become a child in spirit if we are to understand what the kingdom of God is about, let alone to enter it. We have all been children so we can think back to childhood. And there are children around us everywhere so we can watch and study them. And a love of children will unlock the simple profound mystery of which our Lord speaks.

INSIGHTS FROM SCRIPTURE

The essential qualification
Let the children come to me, do not hinder them; for to such belongs the kingdom of God. Truly, I say to you, whoever does not receive the kingdom of God like a child shall not enter it.   *Mark 10:14–15*

Some who qualified
I thank thee, Father, Lord of heaven and earth, that thou hast hidden these things from the wise and understanding and revealed them to babes.   *Luke 10:21*

Truth via simplicity
Have you never read, 'Out of the mouths of babes and sucklings thou hast brought perfect praise'?
                                            Matthew 21:16

A terrible remorse
Whoever receives one such child in my name receives me; but whoever causes one of these little ones who believe in me to sin, it would be better for him to have a great millstone fastened round his neck and to be drowned in the depth of the sea.   *Matthew 18:5–6*

Fearlessness
And a little child shall lead them.   *Isaiah 11:6*

OTHER INSIGHTS

Children in our midst
To hold a baby in one's arms, to lift a child or to put one's
arm around him, to see the wonder in his eyes, to answer his
simple questions, to observe his trust and lack of fear, is to
understand something of the Kingdom. Most of us will have
lost the innocence of childhood, but by quietly observing
children we can confirm our Lord's insight. What we once
knew in innocence and then lost or despised, we can now
know in experience. We have to come back to our beginning
and perhaps understand it for the first time.

Always a child
Our Lord recalls us to our original being, our intimate
being. We are children of God all through our lives, however young, however old, however experienced or dis-
illusioned. We have to return to this original being, assured
now of what we first felt in unquestioning intuition or
received trustingly from others.

Science and the childlike spirit
Sit down before the facts as a little child; be prepared to
give up every preconceived notion, follow humbly and to
whatever abysses nature leads, or you shall learn nothing.
                                            Thomas Huxley

Reverence for children
Inadequate love in childhood or wrong treatment by
parents, teachers or even playmates, often manifests itself in
later life in spiritual or psychological disturbances. The way
to healing lies in trying to recapture the hidden memories
and emotions of the early experiences. The sufferer is
helped to become a child once more and the truth he sees

sets him free. In all our relationships with little ones – our own children, grandchildren, pupils or children we meet – we must give them respect, love, value, and so contribute towards future as well as present happiness.

PRAYERS

The heart of a child

> Grant me, O God,
>   the heart of a child,
> pure and transparent as a spring;
>   a simple heart,
> which never harbours sorrows;
> a heart glorious in self-giving,
>   tender in compassion;
> a heart faithful and generous,
> which will never forget any good
> or bear a grudge for any evil.
>
>   Make me a heart gentle and humble,
> - loving without asking any return,
>   largehearted and undauntable,
> which no ingratitude can sour
> and no indifference can weary;
>   a heart penetrated by the love of Jesus
>   whose desire will only be
>   satisfied in heaven.
>
> Grant me, O Lord,
>   the mind and heart
>   of thy dear Son.

The single eye

Grant me, O Lord, the single eye, that I may see the one thing needful, the thing that you want done. Don't let my vision be blurred by looking at too many things or trying to please anyone but you. Give me simplicity of heart, quiet confidence in you, and eagerness to know and do your will, like your beloved Son, Jesus Christ, my beloved Brother and Lord.

A child in soul
Quietly may I love, quietly obey, quietly pray; quietly and honestly bear my witness, generously think and speak, never seeking to impress or be clever. Thou, O Father, hast set a little Child in our midst: make me a child in soul, a child in purity, a child like that Holy Child, more, more and ever more.   *Eric Milner-White*

Abba, Father! Father, dear Father!

23. TRUST LIFE

If the universe was created by God and human life planned by God, then we should see principles of goodness and wisdom embedded in both. The writer of the book of Genesis pictures God looking at his creation and finding it good. He is emphatic that man is akin to God, made in the divine image. He is conscious of man's ignorance, foolishness and wilfulness, but never does he think of man as being so depraved as not to be able to hear God speaking within himself. There may be a lot of original sin but there is also original goodness to which God and men can appeal. In spite of occasional natural catastrophes, for most of the time we think life is good. So we can trust life, both empirically from experience, and also because we trust the Creator.

INSIGHTS FROM SCRIPTURE

All is good
The generative forces of the world are wholesome, there is no destructive poison in them; and the dominion of Hades is not on earth.   *Wisdom 1:14*

Light in life itself
In him was life, and the life was the light of men. The light
shines in the darkness, and the darkness has not overcome it.
John 1 : 4–5

Guidance assured
Your ears shall hear a word behind you, saying, 'This is the
way, walk in it,' when you turn to the right or when you
turn to the left. *Isaiah 30 : 21*

An inner covenant
I will put my law within them, and I will write it upon their
hearts. *Jeremiah 31 : 33*

Even under trial
The Holy Spirit will teach you in that very hour what you
ought to say. *Luke 12 : 12*

Everything is ours
Everything belongs to you! . . . For you belong to Christ,
and Christ belongs to God. *1 Corinthians 3 : 21–23*
(Phillips)

OTHER INSIGHTS

All belongs to us
The whole world is ours, the whole of life, present and future,
scientific knowledge, artistic beauty, politics, eating and
drinking, sexual love, family life, friendship, justice, nature,
the technical world, philosophy in its true humility as love
of wisdom, daring to ask all the ultimate questions. All
belong to us – conditioned only by one thing, that we belong
to Christ, the Christ whose cross is foolishness and weakness
to the world. We must not be afraid to accept what is given
us, we must not try to escape life. If we know what it means
to be Christ's we shall know how to use and control life.
via Paul Tillich

Exciting and beautiful

And, when the years have all passed, there will gape the
uncomfortable and unpredictable dark void of death, and
into this I shall at last fall headlong, down and down and
down, and the prospect of that fall, that uprooting, that
rending apart of body and spirit, that taking off into so
blank an unknown, drowns me in mortal fear and mortal
grief. After all, life, for all its agonies of despair and loss
and guilt, is exciting and beautiful, amusing and artful and
endearing, full of liking and of love, at times a poem and a
high adventure, at times noble and at times very gay; and
whatever (if anything) is to come after it, we shall not have
this life again.   *Rose Macaulay*

Banishing fear

True faith is an openness to new possibilities, a trust that the
power at work in the universe is a benevolent and loving one.
This calls for the banishing of fear, through the quiet
assurance that love casts out fear; it must continue long
enough to convince the person feared that there is no reciprocal fear or aggressive intention.

PRAYERS

Ready for life and beyond

O God of creating love, help me to be ready for life, open to
its powers and possibilities, eager for its adventures, even
for the final adventure of death that will take me over into
more and higher life, to enjoy the good things which you
have prepared for all whom you love and who will accept
the lovely things you offer, both now and in eternity.

The spiritual power of matter

Blessed be you, harsh matter, barren soil, stubborn rock:
you who yield only to violence, you who force us to work if
we would eat. Blessed be you, perilous matter, violent sea,
untameable passion: you who unless we fetter you will
devour us. Blessed be you, mighty matter, irresistible march

of evolution, reality ever new-born; you who, by constantly shattering our mental categories, force us to go ever further and further in our pursuit of the truth. Blessed be you, universal matter, immeasurable time, boundless ether, triple abyss of stars and atoms and generations: you who by overflowing and dissolving our narrow standards or measurement reveal to us the dimensions of God.

Teilhard de Chardin

Divine surgery may be needed
>   If I have faltered more or less
>   In my great task of happiness;
>   If I have moved among my race
>   And shown no glorious morning face;
>   If beams from happy human eyes
>   Have moved me not; if morning skies,
>   Books and my food, and summer rain
>   Knocked on my sullen heart in vain;
>   Lord, thy most pointed treasure take
>   And stab my spirit broad awake;
>   Or, Lord, if too obdurate I,
>   Choose thou, before that spirit die,
>   A piercing pain, a killing sin,
>   And to my dead heart run them in!

Robert Louis Stevenson

Blessed be thou, O God, for the lovely world, for the animal creation, for my fellow-men, for the joys of life and the hope of lovelier things ahead.

24. SEEK THE TRUTH

Pilate's question 'What is truth?' was a serious one, and one which many a judge has asked when trying to decide a case. It can refer to a statement or account. It can also mean conformity with fact, agreement with reality. More deeply still truth can mean reality, the ultimate meaning of existence, the primary source from which everything else derives. In modern life advertisement and propaganda may have little connection with the facts, while often a man wishes to create a favourable image of himself, whether this is true to his inmost being or not.

INSIGHTS FROM SCRIPTURE

A divine requirement
Behold, thou desirest truth in the inward being; therefore teach me wisdom in my secret heart.   *Psalm 51:6*

The source of truth
Oh send out thy light and thy truth; let them lead me, let them bring me to thy holy hill and to thy dwelling!
Psalm 43:3

The ultimate truth
Grace and truth came through Jesus Christ. No one has ever seen God; the only Son, who is in the bosom of the Father, he has made him known.   *John 1:17–18*

Truth liberates
You will know the truth, and the truth will make you free.
John 8:32

OTHER INSIGHTS

Truth is in a Person
Truth is the perfect correlation of mind and reality; and this is actualized in the Lord's person. If the gospel is true and God is, as the Bible declares, a living God, the ultimate truth is not a system of propositions grasped by a perfect intelligence, but is a personal being apprehended in the only way in which persons are ever fully apprehended, that is, by love.   *William Temple*

Getting near to truth

It is true that what I can apprehend of truth is conditioned and limited by the physical and mental capacities which as a human being I possess. It is true that my knowledge is conditioned by the civilization in which I have been born and its outlook on the world embodied and transmitted to me in the language which I speak. But none the less I find evidence of a remarkable progress in man's understanding of the world. I see the monumental achievement of modern science. I find in history great traditions expressing a worthy, satisfying and noble way of life. I therefore commit myself to the right to criticize them with a view to improving them.
                                                          J. H. Oldham

Passion for truth

Any human being can penetrate to the kingdom of truth, if only he longs for truth and perpetually concentrates all his attention upon its attainment.
                                                          Simone Weil

PRAYERS

Sins against truth

O God, who desirest truth in the inmost heart, forgive me my sins against truth – the untruth within me, the half-lies, the evasions, the exaggerations, the lying silences, the self-deceits, the masks I wear before the world. Let me stand naked before thee, and see myself as I really am. Then grant me truth in the inward parts and keep me in truth always.

Speaking the truth in love

O Lord, grant all who contend for the faith, never to injure it by clamour or impatience; but speaking thy precious truth in love, so to present it that it may be loved and that men may see in it thy goodness and beauty.
                                                          William Bright

Delight in truth
When I found truth, there I found my God who is the truth. And there since the time I learned thee, thou abidest in my memory; and there I find thee, whensoever I call thee to remembrance, and delight in thee.   *St Augustine*

Blessed art thou, my God, the source of all truth, the meaning of all things, the ingathering of all souls. Blessed from the beginning, blessed now and blessed to all eternity.

25. LOVE

Love is not only essential from the point of view of divine command, but also from the angle of human need. People need love and without it they are unfulfilled. A child deprived of love in his early years is not only unhappy at the time, but may suffer spiritual and psychological disturbance in adult years. Old people may be lonely and feel unloved and so unwanted. It is serious not to be loved, and to suffer later from that deprivation. It is equally serious, perhaps more so, not to be able to love. But nothing need stop us from moving out to love other people. And love begets love in return.

INSIGHTS FROM SCRIPTURE

Learnt from Jesus
God is love, and he who abides in love abides in God, and God abides in him.   *1 John 4:16*

Love is eternal
We know that we have passed out of death into life, because we love the brethren.   *1 John 3:14*

No limit to love
A new commandment I give to you, that you love one another; even as I have loved you.   *John 13:34*

Job description
Love is very patient, very kind. Love knows no jealousy; love makes no parade, gives itself no airs, is never rude, never selfish, never irritated, never resentful; love is never glad when others go wrong, love is gladdened by goodness, always slow to expose, always eager to believe the best, always hopeful, always patient. Love never disappears.
1 Corinthians 13:4–8 (Moffatt)

OTHER INSIGHTS

The supreme force
To say that God is love means, amongst other things, that every purpose or policy which is hostile to love, which rests on selfishness, is bound to end in disaster, for it is opposing the supreme principle of existence; and that every purpose or policy which is akin to love is bound to succeed, through whatever sacrifices it may first pass. Therefore it is fighting in alliance with the supreme power.   *William Temple*

Opening up to love
We can never know God by seeking to grasp and mani-pulate him, but only by letting him grasp us . . . by be-coming open to his infinite being which is within us and above us and around us.   *John Macquarrie*

Invincible love
(Two detectives are discussing a young murderer who is being shielded by an elderly aunt.) 'I know it,' he said. 'She'll forgive him without question, whatever he's done to her and however high we hang him. *And he knows it.* It's no use you blaming her. She can't help herself. She's only a vehicle. That's Disinterested Love, Chum, a force, like nuclear energy. It's absolute.'   *Margery Allingham*
                                              'Hide My Eyes'

The two great commands
He is not to be gotten or holden by thought, but only by love.   *The Cloud of Unknowing*

In the darkness
Walking in the dark is a great act of faith. Often it can only
be done in small, feeling steps. At other times we can only
be still and wait for day to come. Travellers by air on a day
of thick dark clouds will know the delighted surprise when
the plane cuts upward through the clouds into the never-
ending sunshine.

Where there is no love, pour love in, and you will draw out
love.   *St John of the Cross*

PRAYERS

Love for love
Grant, O Lord, that thine unimaginable love may find in
me some love to meet it. Let me love the love that ever loves
me . . . that my soul's delight may be to love thee and what
thou lovest, and whom thou lovest, as thou lovest, now and
always, life without end.   *Eric Milner-White*

Love to all
O thou source of all love, let thy love go out to all created
beings, to those I love and to those who love me, to the few
I know and to the many I do not know, to all of every race,
to all the living in this world and to all the living dead in
the next world: may all be free from evil and from harm,
may all come to know thy love and to find the happiness of
loving thee and their fellows. O let the small love of my
heart go out with thine all-embracing love for the sake of
him, who first loved us and taught us love, even Jesus
Christ, our Lord.

Inexorable love
O God of love, I know that your love is so holy and strong
that it cannot acquiesce in anything that is imperfect and
second-rate in those whom you love. I know that your love
will not yield to any prayer of mine that is selfish or unloving.

Let the pure fire of your love burn up in me all that is foreign to your love and holiness, so that I may begin to love like him who taught us love, even Jesus Christ, your beloved Son, and our beloved Lord.

Blessed be thou, O God, Source of love, Giver of love, Demander of love.

26. KEEP STEADY

There are times when it is easy to pray, when there is a sense of God's presence near, when the heart is warm with the memory of past mercies. There are other times when the spirit seems cold and dead, when there is no warmth of emotion or help from memory. All that is left is cold, bare will. But this is the offering most welcome to God, because it is so difficult to give. We keep quiet and steady in the darkness of soul, and before long the brightness of God breaks through the cloud, and faith is stronger for the test it has endured.

INSIGHTS FROM SCRIPTURE

A searching question
Why are you cast down, O my soul, and why are you disquieted within me? Hope in God; for I shall again praise him, my help and my God.   *Psalm 42:11*

Dry and weary
O God, thou art my God, I seek thee, my soul thirsts for thee; my flesh faints for thee, as in a dry and weary land where no water is.   *Psalm 63:1*

Jesus was not exempt
My God! My God! why hast thou forsaken me?
                                        Mark 15:34

Wait patiently
I waited patiently for the Lord; he inclined to me and
heard my cry. He drew me up from the desolate pit, out of
the miry bog, and set my feet upon a rock, making my steps
secure.   *Psalm 40 : 1–2*

OTHER INSIGHTS

True faith
That man is perfect in faith who can come to God in the
utter dearth of his feelings and desires, without a glow or an
aspiration, with the weight of low thoughts, failures,
neglects, and wandering forgetfulness, and say to him,
'Thou art my refuge'.   *George Macdonald*

The cloud between
For at the first time thou findest but a darkness and, as it
were, a cloud of unknowing, thou knowest not what, savest
that thou feelest in thy will a naked intent unto God. This
darkness and this cloud is betwixt thee and thy God, and
telleth thee that thou mayest neither see him clearly by
light of understanding, nor feel him in sweetness of love in
thine affection, and therefore shape thee to bide in this
darkness as long as thou mayest, crying after him that thou
lovest . . . Then he will sometimes peradventure send a beam
of ghostly light piercing this cloud of unknowing that is
betwixt thee and him, and show thee some of his privity of
the which man may not nor cannot speak.
                              The Cloud of Unknowing

PRAYERS

Question and answer
O my Lord, when moods of depression, anxiety, or resent-
ment take possession of me, train me to ask, 'Why art thou
so heavy, O my soul, and why art thou so disquieted
within me?' And let the answer show me the cause of my
mood and dispel it, so that I forget my hurts and want only
thee.

My own wilderness
Give me that tranquil courage which is content to await your gift. I live by what comes to me from you. Your word proceeding forth from your mouth, at your own time, in your way: not by my deliberate self-occupied use of the power you give. Sometimes my need and exhaustion seem very great, and you seem very silent: surrounding conditions seem very stony, and hard. Those are the moments when my faith is purified, when I am given my chance of patience and fortitude and tranquillity: abiding among the stones in the wilderness and learning the perfection of dependence on you.

Evelyn Underhill

Waiting for a shower
When the heart is hard and parched up, come upon me with a shower of mercy. When grace is lost from life, come with a burst of song. When tumultuous work raises its din on all sides shutting me out from beyond, come to me, my lord of silence, with thy peace and rest. When my beggarly heart sits crouched, shut up in a corner, break open the door, my king, and come with the ceremony of a king. When desire blinds the mind with delusion and dust, O thou holy one, thou wakeful, come with thy light and thy thunder.

Rabindranath Tagore

Lighten our darkness, we beseech thee, O Lord, and by thy great mercy defend us from all the perils and dangers of our spiritual night.

27. INTEGRITY

What do we mean when we speak of a man of integrity? One who will be true to the highest he knows; who will never betray the truth or trifle with it; one who will never make a decision from self-regarding motives; one who will never yield to the persuasion of friends or the pressure of critics unless either conforms to his own standards of right and wrong; one who will face the consequences of his attitudes, decisions and actions, however costly they may be; one who will not be loud in self-justification, but quietly confident and humbly ready to explain.

INSIGHTS FROM SCRIPTURE

In the face of opposition
(All this we want to meet) with sincerity, with insight and patience . . . with genuine love, speaking the plain truth, and living by the power of God. Our sole defence, our only weapon, is a life of integrity, whether we meet honour or dishonour, praise or blame.   *2 Corinthians 6:6–8*
(Phillips)

An example of integrity
Have you considered my servant Job, that there is none like him on the earth, a blameless and upright man, who fears God and turns away from evil? He still holds fast his integrity.   *Job 2:3*

A definition of integrity
Who shall ascend the hill of the Lord? And who shall stand in his holy place? He who has clean hands and a pure heart, who does not lift up his soul to what is false, and does not swear deceitfully.   *Psalm 24:3–4*

Guide to integrity
Not every one who says to me, 'Lord, Lord,' shall enter the

kingdom of heaven, but he who does the will of my Father
who is in heaven.   *Matthew 7 : 21*

OTHER INSIGHTS

Pseudo-goodness
Pseudo-goodness will prefer routine duty to courage and
creativity. In the end it will be content with established
procedures and safe formulas, while turning a blind eye to
the greatest enormities of injustice and uncharity. Such are
the routines of piety that sacrifice everything else to preserve the comforts of the past, however inadequate and
shameful they may be in the present. Meditation, in such a
case, becomes a factory for alibis, and instead of struggling
with the sense of falsity and inauthenticity in oneself, it
battles against the exigencies of the present with platitudes
minted in the previous century. If necessary it also fabri-
cates condemnations and denunciations of those who risk
new ideas and new solutions.   *Thomas Merton*

Gospel lineaments
> A sweet attractive kind of grace,
> A full assurance borne by looks,
> Continual comfort in a face,
> The lineaments of Gospel books.
>   *A friend's description of Sir Philip Sidney*

How often, like Ananias and Sapphira, we profess to give
everything to God, and keep back part, either knowingly
or in self-deception. Both the willed cheating and the unrecognized insincerity are warnings of mortal disease in the
soul. Father-confessors in the past were right in speaking of
deadly sins, the real killers of spiritual life, unless detected
and treated by true penitence which involves self-knowledge, humble confession, acceptance of forgiveness and
intention of amendment by the help of God's grace.

PRAYERS

An upright heart
Give me, O Lord, a steadfast heart, which no unworthy
thought can drag downwards, an unconquered heart, which
no tribulation can wear out; an upright heart, which no
unworthy purpose may tempt aside. Bestow upon me also,
O Lord my God, understanding to know thee, diligence to
seek thee, wisdom to find thee, and a faithfulness that may
finally embrace thee; through Jesus Christ our Lord.

Thomas Aquinas

The Spirit's X-ray
O Lord and Master, who dost know us more truly than we
know ourselves: let thy Holy Spirit search out our weaknesses, our fears, the unsurrendered things within our souls,
that we may be saved from denial, offence, disloyalty, and
betrayal, and be of whole heart in our commitment to thee.

No foothold for evil
O Christ our Lord, who wast in all things tempted as we are,
yet more searchingly and subtly by the spirit of evil, trying
to deflect thee from the perfect will of the Father; make
clear to us his evil intent and deliver us from his power;
that as he found nothing in thee so he may gain no foothold
in us who invoke thy victory and thy grace to be our rescue
and our strength until the final triumph, O Christ our Lord.

O God, give me integrity of heart and holiness of character
that I may feel at home in thy presence.

28. SERENITY

Sometimes we meet a person who has a quiet serenity of spirit of which we become quickly conscious; who seems to be unhurried and unworried; uncomplaining about the past, content with the present, unafraid of the future; one who seems to live in another tempo of life, with a stillness that is not a technique but comes from a centre of stillness within himself; one who is relaxed and restful, unself-assertive; whose 'isness' says more than his words, and will validate his words when he speaks of what he has discovered.

INSIGHTS FROM SCRIPTURE

A prophet's prayer
Thou dost keep him in perfect peace, whose mind is stayed on thee, because he trusts in thee.   *Isaiah 26:3*

A psalmist's experience
I have calmed and quieted my soul, like a child quieted at its mother's breast; like a child that is quieted is my soul.
Psalm 131:2

A king's last words
He dawns on them like the morning light, like the sun shining forth upon a cloudless morning, like rain that makes grass to sprout from the earth.   *2 Samuel 23:4*

An apostle's promise
And the peace of God, which passes all understanding, will keep your hearts and your minds in Christ Jesus.
Philippians 4:7

OTHER INSIGHTS

Complete trust
Teach us stillness and confident peace
In thy perfect will,
Deep calm of soul, and content
In what thou wilt do with these lives thou has given.

Teach us to wait and be still,
To rest in thyself,
To hush this clamorous anxiety,
To lay in thine arms all this wealth thou has given.

J. S. Hoyland

The umpire within
Let every inward debate between self and God, between
self and others, be ruled and guided by the deep consciousness that in Christ you are indeed at rest: let the plea for
self-assertion be ever met and negatived by the decision of
that umpire in favour of love.

C. Moule

Radiating peace
There is a lovely devotional practice in Buddhism in which
the devout Buddhist sits in quiet meditation and radiates
to all living beings love, joy, compassion and peace in turn.
The Christian can well follow this example by sending out
his own peace of heart to those nearest to him, to all who are
worried and troubled or in the grip of enmity or hatred,
reinforced by the infinitely more generous and effective
peace of God, for which he offers himself as a channel,
both in prayer and in life.

PRAYERS

Grant unto us, O Lord, the royalty of inward happiness and
the serenity which comes from living close to thee. Daily
renew in us the sense of joy, and let thy eternal Spirit dwell

in our souls and bodies, filling every corner of our hearts with light and gladness. So that bearing about with us the infection of a good courage we may be diffusers of life, and meet all that comes of good or ill, even death itself, with gallant and true-hearted happiness, giving thee thanks always for all things, through Jesus Christ our Lord.

Order of St Michael and St George

Regarding the world
      God grant me the serenity
      To accept the things I cannot change,
      The courage to change the things I can,
      And the wisdom to know the difference.

Reinhold Niebuhr

A tranquil mind
Grant me, O God, tranquillity of mind and soul out of a faith settled and lively, secure from the world's fevers, serene in the knowledge of thy nearness, and of thy perfect, unchanging will; dwelling in the light eternal and the truth invisible, aglow with Christ's Spirit, and Christ's love.

Eric Milner-White

Blessed be thou, O Christ, my Master – never hurried, never worried, always trusting the goodness, the wisdom and the love of God.

V. WHAT OBSTACLES?

*What forces are working against me,
and how may I overcome them?*

29. SELF-EVALUATION

Implicit in the command to love one's neighbour as one's self is the duty to love one's self, safeguarded by an equal love of neighbour. Each soul is valued and loved by God, and its individuality or divine image respected. Some people overvalue themselves in pride and self-confidence, though both of these self-regarding characteristics may spring from a hidden doubt. Others undervalue themselves and shrink from openness or helpful initiative to other people. The secret of mature balance will be to accept ourselves as we are and not try to imitate others, and then to rely on God's grace to build us up to the best of which we are capable.

INSIGHTS FROM SCRIPTURE

A disciple's potential
So you are Simon the son of John? You shall be called Cephas (which means a rock).   *John 1:42*

A king's failure
God gave him another heart.   *1 Samuel 10:9*

Now the Spirit of the Lord departed from Saul, and an evil spirit from the Lord troubled him.   *1 Samuel 16:14*

An apostle's experience
If any one is in Christ, he is a new creation; the old has passed away, behold, the new has come.

2 Corinthians 5:17

A son's return
But when he came to himself he said, ' . . . I will arise and go to my father, and I will say to him, "Father, I have sinned against heaven and before you; I am no longer worthy to be called your son." '   *Luke 15:17–19*

OTHER INSIGHTS

Naked before God
We hide from God, we hide from one another and cover ourselves with all kinds of ethical, intellectual and spiritual garments, because we are ashamed to be found naked; we hide from ourselves, putting lofty screens around our thoughts. Now the first thing the Bible does for us is to uncover all our hiding places and wrappings; we have to stand before God as we are, we have to see ourselves in that crude light.   *Suzanne de Dietrich*

Wrestling with one's self
Jacob had been running away all his life – from Esau whom he had cheated, from Laban whom he had deceived. There comes a moment when he can no longer evade an encounter. He spends the night in wrestling with himself. 'What is your name?' he is asked by a mysterious opponent in a nightmare dream, to which he replies, 'My name is Jacob (a twister).' This frank recognition gains a new name 'Israel' – one who has struggled with God and won through.

Growing knowledge of self
Paul in his great hymn of love speaks of our present partial knowledge and holds out the hope of knowing and understanding as fully as God now knows and understands me. This coming to self-knowledge is the beginning of maturity and salvation. It is the God of love who knows me fully and his will is that I shall progress towards the perfection of his will for me.

PRAYERS

My inner life
O Lord God, I thank thee for the growing knowledge of myself, of the depths of personality which affect my thinking, my feeling, my behaviour, and my dreams. There is so much

more than I ever thought, so much more to offer thee for the cleansing and sanctifying of thy Spirit. Heal my inner divisions in the unity of thy will, set my fears at rest in the assurance of thy love and grace, let no resentments destroy my inner peace, no thoughts of self deflect me from thy purpose for me. Help me to grow towards the fullness of life and love seen in thy blessed Son, Jesus Christ my Lord.

From death to life
I know that I have passed from death unto life. No more am I enclosed in myself; no more feed on the imaginations of pride nor brood on the slights to it: gone are self-conscious terrors and timidities, gone the aimlessness and petty judgements.

I know that I have passed from death unto life.

Eric Milner-White

All for my growth
Let me depend on God alone: who never changes, who knows what is best for me so much better than I; and gives in a thousand ways, at all times, all that the perfect Father can for the son's good growth – things needful, things salutary, things wise, beneficent and happy.

Eric Milner-White

O Lord, I thank thee that in bringing me to what I really am thou dost bring me to thyself.

30. SELF-CENTREDNESS

It is almost inevitable that each of us should in some degree think of himself as a central point. A small child growing in consciousness naturally and delightfully thinks of everyone and everything as related to himself. As he grows he gradually realizes that others think of themselves in the same way and so has to learn adjustment. A self-centred person is difficult to live with, and a person full of himself will have no room for God. Heaven is the perfection of love, and selfishness can have no place there.

INSIGHTS FROM SCRIPTURE

Self-preservation is counter-productive
If any man would come after me, let him deny himself and take up his cross and follow me. For whoever would save his life will lose it, and whoever loses his life for my sake shall find it.   *Matthew 16 : 24–25*

The true self is priceless
What will a man gain by winning the whole world, at the cost of his true self? Or what can he give that will buy that self back?   *Matthew 16 : 26* (NEB)

The old self is dead
We know that our old self was crucified with him so that the sinful body might be destroyed, and we might no longer be enslaved to sin.   *Romans 6 : 6*

A new centre
I have been crucified with Christ; it is no longer I who live, but Christ who lives in me; and the life I now live in the flesh I live by faith in the Son of God, who loved me and gave himself for me.   *Galatians 2 : 20*

OTHER INSIGHTS

A higher loyalty
To be faithful to the God of justice and mercy is to be faithless to self-centredness and pride in oneself; to be perpetually faithless to the inner dishonesties and deceits, the subterfuges and escapes, the covert rebellion and inner idols.   *Paul Minear*

The only safe centre
If a man is centred upon himself the smallest risk is too great
for him, because both success and failure can destroy him.
If he is centred upon God, then no risk is too great, because
success is already guaranteed – the successful union of
Creator and creature, beside which everything else is
meaningless.

Morris West
'The Shoes of the Fisherman'

Hemmed in
Edith was a little country bounded on north and south and
east and west by Edith.

Killing the nerve
No grasping or seeking, no hungering of the individual, shall
give motion to the will: no desire to be conscious of worthi-
ness shall order the life; no ambition whatever shall be a
motive of action; no wish to surpass another be allowed a
moment's respite from death.

George Macdonald

PRAYERS

The true cross
O Christ, my Lord, you tell me that I am to take up my
cross and follow you. Help me to know that it is a cross laid
on me by you, and not a cross of my own, made by lack of
holiness or love. If it is a true cross, grant me acceptance,
quiet trust in you, and courage. If it is of my own making,
make me see the cause which produced it, and nail the old
self to it, so that dying with you, I may have your risen life,
your values, your attitudes, your desire for the Father's will,
and your obedience to it, O Lord of all true crosses.

Displacing self
Lord, bestow on me two gifts – to forget myself, – never to
forget thee. Keep me from self-love, self-pity, self-will, in
every guise and disguise, nor ever let me measure myself by
myself, but only by thy Son, true Son of Man and very God.

Eric Milner-White

In a new milieu
Lord, enfold me in the depths of your heart; and there hold
me, refine, purge, and set me on fire, raise me aloft, until my
own self knows utter annihilation.   *Teilhard de Chardin*

> To my God a heart of flame;
> To my fellow-men a heart of love;
> To myself a heart of steel.   *St Augustine*

31. IMMATURITY

Many of us do not grow in inner health and maturity as we
grow in bodily health, mental ability and control over outside things. Few of us devote to the study of God and his will
the same time and application that we give to worldly
studies and professional training. The writers of the New
Testament frequently lament the lack of maturity in the
Christians for whom they are writing. That spiritual
maturity is essential for inner health, right attitudes and
right decisions and is creative for a dimension of life beyond
the physical and the material.

INSIGHTS FROM SCRIPTURE

Conception
My little children, with whom I am again in travail until
Christ be formed in you!   *Galatians 4 : 19*

Growth
Like newborn babes, long for the pure spiritual milk, that
by it you may grow up to salvation; for you have tasted
the kindness of the Lord.   *1 Peter 2 : 2–3*

Maturity
Until we all attain to the unity of the faith and of the

knowledge of the Son of God, to mature manhood, to the measure of the stature of the fullness of Christ.

Ephesians 4 : 13

The will is weak

For I know that nothing good dwells within me, that is, in my flesh. I can will what is right, but I cannot do it. For I do not do the good I want, but the evil I do not want is what I do.

Romans 7 : 18–19

OTHER INSIGHTS

Only silly

O God, dear God, if so be you do exist, hear me. I know they say there isn't a hell, but if there is, O God, dear God, kind God, don't let Ray burn. He was only silly, O God, dear God, only stinkingly silly. Don't let him burn.

Margery Allingham
(A schoolboy's prayer for his murdered stepfather in 'Fashion in Shrouds')

The mature person

Mature people are independent of the fads, fashions and prejudices of those around them. They lead individual lives, yet work harmoniously and efficiently with others. They know when to conform and when not to. They know how to avoid the polarities of collectivism and individualism. They take people for what they are in themselves, rather than for what their colour, race or class is. They have a sense of humour and are able to laugh at the vicissitudes and absurdities of life, including their own foibles. They can detect humbug and cant and are merely amused by pomposity and self-importance. They live in the moment and have an awareness of present things. They do not dwell on past regrets or future fears. They can communicate easily and so form deep relationships. Such people strike others as creative, harmonious, intelligent and understanding.

Martin Israel

The model
In him we find model for our every word and deed, moving or standing, seated, eating, silent or speaking, alone or with others. Study him and thou wilt grow in his love, in his company. Thou wilt gain sweetness and confidence and thou wilt be strengthened in every virtue. Let this be thy wisdom, this thy meditation, this thy study, to have him always in mind to move thee to imitation, to win thee to his love.   *Archbishop Goodier*

PRAYERS

For new birth
Father, let me be born in thee as thy child: Christ, be born in me as my Lord: Holy Spirit, travail and shine within; that I may live in thy life and love with thy love evermore and evermore.   *Eric Milner-White*

For maturity and holiness
O God, I recognize that my sins are spiritual sickness, selfishness, incompleteness, immaturity, falling short of your will and your glory. Let your grace heal me, make me selfless, lead me to maturity and holiness, complete me, according to the pattern of your unique Son, Jesus Christ, my Lord.

Christification
Strengthen, O Lord, the progress of Christification in the spirits of men, by new insights of truth, further impulses to goodness, growing maturity within, a deeper, wider love of our fellow-men, as well as by our willed communion with you and our experience of your Spirit at work in our spirits, so that we may grow to the true humanity seen in Jesus Christ, our Lord.

O Lord, when I awake up after thy likeness, I shall be satisfied with it.   *Psalm 17:16* (BCP)

32. WORRY

Many people seem to think that worry is an expression of virtuous concern. On the contrary it is a subtle sin for it amounts to a distrust of God – his love, his will, his grace. Moreover, it makes one confused in mind and unable to think clearly. We should take any quiet forethought possible, and then trust God to guide and strengthen us to meet each duty, difficulty or emergency, as and when it comes.

INSIGHTS FROM SCRIPTURE

A prophet's assurance
Thou dost keep him in perfect peace, whose mind is stayed on thee, because he trusts in thee.   *Isaiah 26 : 3*

Our Lord's confidence
Do not be anxious, saying, 'What shall we eat?' or 'What shall we drink?' or 'What shall we wear?' . . . your heavenly Father knows that you need all these things.
                                           Matthew 6 : 31–32

An apostle's advice
Cast all your anxieties on him, for he cares about you.
                                           1 Peter 5 : 7

Turn it into trusting prayer
Have no anxiety about anything, but in everything by prayer and supplication with thanksgiving let your requests be made known to God.   *Philippians 4 : 6*

OTHER INSIGHTS

Look at the birds
        The birds that fly in the open sky
        They neither toil nor spin,

They build no barns to store their grain,
  Yet God takes care of them;
And you, O man, through eternity's span
  Are infinitely dear to him.

Use the lift

In many airports, railway stations and big stores there are moving staircases to take people and their baggage from one level to another. The wise traveller puts down his suitcases on the stairway and lets it carry them for him. So we rest our burdens on the Lord, who is ready to carry our anxieties and griefs, if we will let him.

Turn cares into prayers

The release of anxiety is to turn cares into prayers. If we feel anxious about somebody, ill or in danger or need, that anxiety does no good to us or to them. But if that anxiety is turned into a prayer, it widens and enriches our spiritual life, it turns a thought which is depressing into a thought which is uplifting, and it helps the person we are praying for.

Geoffrey Harding

PRAYERS

Heavy burdens

O blessed Jesu Christ, who didst bid all who carry heavy burdens to come to thee, refresh us with thy presence and thy power. Quiet our understandings and give ease to our hearts, by bringing us close to things infinite and eternal. Open to us the mind of God, that in his light we may see light. And crown thy choice of us to be thy servants, by making us springs of strength and joy to all whom we serve.

Evelyn Underhill

Inner peace

Dear Lord, quieten my spirit and fix my thoughts on thy will, that I may see what thou wouldest have done, and contemplate its doing without self-consciousness or inner excitement, without haste and without delay, without fear of other people's judgements or anxiety about success, knowing only that it is thy will and must therefore be done quietly, faithfully, and lovingly, for in thy will alone is our peace.

Quiet hearts
O Spirit of God, set at rest the crowded, hurrying, anxious thoughts within our minds and hearts. Let the peace and quiet of thy presence take possession of us. Help us to rest, to relax, to become open and receptive to thee. Thou dost know our inmost spirits, the hidden unconscious life within us, the forgotten memories of hurts and fears, the frustrated desires, the unresolved tensions and dilemmas. Cleanse and sweeten the springs of our being, that freedom, life and love may flow into both our conscious and hidden life. Lord, we lie open before thee, waiting for thy peace, thy healing, and thy word.

O God, you are my rock, my rescue, and my refuge, I leave it all quietly to you.

33. SHORTFALL

Whenever we see someone doing something superbly well – a tennis player, a pianist, a speaker – our admiration goes out to him, and we envy his ease and skill. Maybe we feel like the Queen of Sheba in the impact of Solomon's superlative wisdom and there is no heart left in us. As we read the gospels we are aware of one who was supremely human, who lived our life with ease and grace, whose love never failed. In the light of that incarnation of life we are conscious of how far short we fall, of the gap that cannot be bridged from our end of it only.

INSIGHTS FROM SCRIPTURE

A realistic admission
All have sinned and fall short of the glory of God.
Romans 3 : 23

An impossible standard?
You, therefore, must be perfect, as your heavenly Father is perfect.   *Matthew 5:48*

A provocative question
All these I have observed; what do I still lack?
                                                                   Matthew 19:20

Comforting answers
Who is sufficient for these things? . . . Our competence is from God . . . My grace is sufficient for you, for my power is made perfect in weakness.   *2 Corinthians 2:16, 3:5, 12:9*

Our main hope
Christ in you, the hope of glory.   *Colossians 1:27*

OTHER INSIGHTS

Insatiate
The more I win thee, Lord, the more for thee, I pine;
     O, such a heart of mine!
My eyes behold thee, and are filled, and straightway then
     Their hunger wakes again!
My arms have clasped thee and should set thee free, but no,
     I cannot let thee go!
Thou dwell'st within my heart, forthwith anew the fire
     Burns of my soul's desire.
Lord Jesus Christ, Beloved, tell, O tell me true,
     What shall thy servant do?   *Tilak,*
                                                     An Indian Christian poet

Never enough
Through all his plunging and restless days ran the refrain:
I have not suffered enough; I have not sacrificed enough;
I am not yet worthy even of the shadow of the crown of
thorns. He wandered about the valleys of the world looking
for the hill that had the outline of a skull.   *G. K. Chesterton*
                                                        'St Francis of Assisi'

A lifetime job
Let no man think that sudden in a minute,
All is accomplished and the work is done;
Though with thine earliest dawn thou should'st begin it,
Scarce were it ended in thy setting sun.

F. W. H. Myers

PRAYERS

Lord, I am mediocre; help thou my mediocrity.

Never enough
Lord, I can never love thee enough, never thank thee
enough, never serve thee enough. Be thou my sufficiency,
that inspired by thee I may do good things, loving things,
and strengthened by thee do difficult things, attempt
impossible things, in thee and for thee, O Lord, my God.

Not worthy
Lord, I am not worthy that thou shouldest come under my
roof, yet I know that I cannot live without thee. Lord, I am
sinful; without thee I cannot become holy. Lord, I am unloving; come to my heart and waken it to love. Lord,
my heart is small; enlarge it, throw it open, that I may
welcome thee and make room for all who come looking for
love.

A long way behind
O my Lord, I realize how far short I fall of your holiness
and love. Yet I see in you the perfection which I long to
attain. Enrol me in your school that I may learn from you.
In your company let me discover how to love and serve my
fellow-men. Reprove me, train me, encourage me, that at
last the disciple may be as his master. Lord and master,
don't despair of me, don't write me off. Without you I am
lost, with you there is hope. Lord, there is no other to
whom I can go; you have the meaning of life in this world
and in the world to come. I am a long way behind, but

wherever I see your footprints, I will plant my own, straining my eyes to see you far ahead, leading me on to the Father
of souls, my Creator and my God.

My mouth shall speak of thy goodness all the day long. For
I know no end thereof and there is no end thereof.

34. LACK OF FAITH

Faith is not knowledge or certainty. It is often contrasted
with reason, but the true contrast is with the evidence of the
senses. Faith is a kind of spiritual sight, an in-seeing into
realities. It always wants to get beyond the superficial
surface of things, into the spiritual behind the material. It
wants to go beyond the outside symptoms into the causes of
them. It consists of following knowledge and reason as far
as they will take us, and then going beyond, in the same
direction. There is a risk about faith, which can only be
tested by taking the leap when the sure path comes to an
end.

INSIGHTS FROM SCRIPTURE

Divine reproaches
Because of your little faith . . . O men of little faith . . .
Where is your faith? . . . Why did you doubt?
>   *Matthew 17:20, Matthew 6:30,*
>   *Luke 8:25, Matthew 14:31*

Faith is spiritual sight
Faith is the assurance of things hoped for, the conviction of
things not seen . . . He endured as seeing him who is invisible . . . We walk by faith, not by sight.
>   *Hebrews 11:1, 11:27, 2 Corinthians 5:7*

Mountains of difficulty
If you have faith as a grain of mustard seed, you will say to

this mountain, 'Move from here to there' and it will move;
and nothing will be impossible to you.   *Matthew 17:20*

Jesus makes faith possible
Looking to Jesus the pioneer and perfector of our faith . . .
I know whom I have believed.
Hebrews 12:1, 2 Timothy 1:12

OTHER INSIGHTS

Adventuring faith

We are the Pilgrims, master; we should go
Always a little further: it may be
Beyond that last blue mountain barred with snow
Across that angry or that glimmering sea . . .

We travel not for trafficking alone;
By hotter winds our fiery hearts are fanned;
For lust of knowing what should not be known,
We take the Golden Road to Samarkand.
James Elroy Flecker
'Hassan'

Faith at its highest
Faith is most faith when it is tempted and threatened: faith
is present when looking at the most difficult situation it says
'Nevertheless', when in the face of every misgiving and
reverse, it continues to say 'My God! My God!'

Ultimate concern
Faith is the fundamental concern in a man's life . . . where
his heart lies, the inner core of his personality, his ultimate
concern, the concern that he thinks to be final, ultimate and
supreme.   *Charles Davis*

If we doubt . . .
If we believe, then everything is illuminated and takes shape
around us: chance is seen to be order, success assumes an
incorruptible plenitude, suffering becomes a visit and a
caress of God. But if we hesitate, the rock remains dry, the

sky dark, the waters treacherous and shifting. And we may hear the voice of the Master, faced with our bungled lives: 'O men of little faith, why have you doubted . . .?'

Teilhard de Chardin

PRAYERS

Joy in believing

O God, who hast created the universe and art ever at work in it to restore the harmony broken by the self-will of men: give us quiet, confident, joyful faith in thee, that our eyes may ever look in expectation to thy love and power, rather than to the power of evil or to the weakness of men. Help us to stand firm in the assurance that thou art at work in all that happens, in the foolishness and rebellion of men as well as in their efforts for goodness, turning all to thy loving purpose. Fill us with joy and hope in believing, through him who was victorious over sin, enmity, defeat, and death, even Jesus Christ, our beloved Lord.

Holding on

O God, I bring this situation to thee and hold it to thee, refusing to let it get away from thee, believing that by thy grace, in answer to my prayer it will change, that something will turn up that was not there before, that the mountain of difficulty will be removed or thy wisdom show me the way to go round or thy grace strengthen me to climb over it or tunnel through it. Let me hold on in faith and love, O Lord my God.

Open my eyes

Open my eyes, O Lord, that I may see the chariots of fire, the crowd of watching angels and saints, the four living creatures of creation, the hosts of the redeemed, from every nation and every generation, and thyself, standing in the place of power, directing thy kingdom and strengthening every struggling follower. So seeing thee, may I be held quiet and unafraid, ready and daring, to be and to do and to experience all that thy loving wisdom allows or wills, O beloved author and finisher of my faith.

> O Lord,
>> Let the mustard seed of faith be in me
>> and let it grow
>> until it permeate
>> my whole life
>>> my outlook
>>>> and my actions.

35. JUST PLAIN SIN

Anyone who from time to time will sit quiet with himself and survey his life and present state will be conscious of failure. He will remember things of which he is now ashamed. He will see his secret selfishness, his carefully controlled ambitions, his secret lusts. He will know the power of temptations – from without and within. He will recognize times of wilful choice of wrong attitudes and deeds. When he compares himself with the perfection of Jesus, he will realize his need of forgiveness, a fresh start and continuing grace.

INSIGHTS FROM SCRIPTURE

Sinful disposition
Out of the heart of man, come evil thoughts, fornication, theft, murder, adultery, coveting, wickedness, deceit, licentiousness, envy, slander, pride, foolishness. All these evil things come from within, and they defile a man.

Mark 7 : 21–23

The antidote
What is good has been explained to you, man; this is what the Lord God asks of you: only this, to act justly, to love tenderly and to walk humbly with your God.

Micah 6 : 8 (Jerusalem Bible)

Wilful perverseness
Woe to those who call evil good and good evil, who put
darkness for light, and light for darkness, who put bitter for
sweet and sweet for bitter!   *Isaiah 5:20*

Breaking God's law
Every one who commits sin is guilty of lawlessness; sin is
lawlessness.   *1 John 3:4*

Re-crucifying Jesus
They crucify to themselves the Son of God afresh, and put
him to an open shame.   *Hebrews 6:6* (AV)

OTHER INSIGHTS

The ultimate result
St Paul says that the wages of sin is death, not that God
condemns us to death for our sins, but that sin kills the life
of the spirit. Sin is a sickness that leads to spiritual death
unless it is cured by forgiveness and the soul kept healthy by
grace.

The wrong centre
Sin is the putting of self in the centre where God alone
should be. Sin is acting from the self instead of from God. It
is falling short of the will and glory of God. Often it is more
than that – it is setting one's will against God's will, consciously (when guilt is involved) or unconsciously (when the
sinful consequences are equally disastrous).

A loyal question
When a troubled, confused disciple asks the question 'Lord,
is it I?' it is clear that it is not he, for he is troubled at the
very thought of betrayal. Yet he is rightly concerned lest
unwittingly he should have betrayed his master.

All sin is grievous
          Sin against Law is grievous indeed;

Sin against Light, even more grievous;
Sin against Love, most grievous of all.

PRAYERS

Confession
Almighty God, my heavenly Father, I have sinned against
thee and my fellow-men, in thought and word and deed,
and in what I have left undone. I am heartily sorry and
repent. For the sake of thy Son, my Lord Jesus Christ,
forgive what I have been, amend what I am, direct what I
shall be; that I may walk in newness of life, to the glory of
thy name.

Purifying fire
O God, I know that thy nature is so pure that it destroys
all that is not pure as fire. I know that the fire does not burn
once in condemnation but that it will continue to burn me
until I am pure, until all that is foreign to it has yielded to
its force, no longer with pain and consuming, but with the
pure light of holiness. O God, I will hold myself in thy
purifying fire.

A Muslim prayer
O God, I knock at the door of thy mercy with the hand of
hope, I flee unto thee, seeking refuge from my multiplied
sins, and I hang upon the borders of thy garment with the
fingers of my trust. So pardon, O God, the wrongs I have
done, the evils and the sins, and rid me, O God, of my evil
state, for thou art my Lord and Sovereign, my reliance and
my hope.   *A Sufi mystic*

The Saviour of all to every man
'Son, your sins are forgiven. Go and sin no more.'

VI. IN THE BEGINNING

How can I discover the ground of all being?
Can I know this power in a personal way?
Can I enter into a living relationship?

36. GOD HIMSELF

In recent years some theologians have told us that God is dead, and some religious people have feared that their faith in God has been shaken. Others have perceived that the way in which people of a past age have expressed their experience and faith is no longer adequate for an age in which we know more about the universe and our inner selves. Our idea of God must change, be enlarged and deepened, yet always governed by the mystery of the divine being.

INSIGHTS FROM SCRIPTURE

Invisible in his essential being
The blessed and only Sovereign, the King of kings, and Lord of lords, who alone has immortality, and dwells in unapproachable light, whom no man has ever seen or can see. *1 Timothy 6 : 15–16*

A to Z
I am the Alpha and the Omega, the beginning and the end.
Revelation 21 : 6

Existence, timeless and personal
If . . . they ask me, 'What is his name?' what shall I say to them? . . . Say this to the people of Israel, 'I AM has sent me to you.' *Exodus 3 : 13–14*

Scriptural affirmations
God is . . . God is Spirit . . . God is Truth . . . God is Light . . . God is Love . . . God is eternal . . . God is the God and Father of Jesus Christ.

One Eternal Reality
I AM is the unqualified fullness of being
     is the supreme indication of presence
     is the one statement that cannot be uttered without
       being completely true
     is the one completely and immediately personal
       statement
     is pre-supposed in every intelligible utterance
     is true equally of God and man
     is true in every time and place
     is the name of God.   *T. S. Gregory*

A Buddhist describes the Ultimate
We are told that Nirvana is permanent, stable, imperishable, unmoveable, ageless, deathless, unborn and un-
become; that it is power, bliss and happiness, the secure
refuge, the shelter and the place of unassailable safety,
that it is the real truth and the Supreme Reality; that it is
the Good, the supreme goal, and the one and only consummation of our life, the eternal, hidden and incompre-
hensible Peace.   *E. Conze* 'Buddhism'

Right to protest
One cannot escape the feeling that what modern atheism
is revolting against is, in part at least, the objectified God,
conceived by the atheists, as by many Christians, as an
immensely magnified human person, with whom men can
talk on human terms and arraign his government of the
world. But that is not God, but an idol and, in so far as
modern atheism destroys that idol, it is doing a service to
true religion.   *J. H. Oldham*

PRAYERS

Beyond all thought
God is what thought cannot better; God is whom thought cannot reach; God no thinking can even conceive. Without God, men can have no being, no reason, no knowledge, no good desire, naught. Thou, O God, art what thou art, transcending all.   *Eric Milner-White*

Words fail
O Thou Supreme! most secret and most present, most beautiful and strong! What shall I say, my God, my Life, my Holy Joy? What shall any man say when he speaks of thee?   *St Augustine*

God seen in Christ
O Thou who art beyond all images, thought-forms and word-expressions, have compassion on us who try to express what we have experienced of thee. We have to think about thee, picture thee, speak of thee; help us to know that we can never grasp thee but only be grasped by thee, never describe thee as object but only experience thee as subject. Forgive the images that we make of thee and grant that each successive one may come closer to that given us by thy blessed Son, Jesus Christ our Lord.

Blessed be thou, O God, beyond all names, all thought, all words, the Supreme and Final Reality in whom we live and move and have our being.

37. CREATOR

The Bible opens with an act of faith, 'In the beginning God created the heaven and the earth.' There is no speculation or argument, only a declaration of faith, followed by the poem of creation, which does not claim to be a historical account or a scientific description but poetry's mystic insight. A New Testament writer echoes this initial act of biblical faith when he says 'By faith we understand that the world was created by the word of God.'   (*Hebrews 11 : 3*)

INSIGHTS FROM SCRIPTURE

Creator Spirit
The earth was without form and void, and darkness was upon the face of the deep; and the Spirit of God was moving over the face of the waters.   *Genesis 1 : 2*

Creative Love
For thou lovest all things that exist . . . for thou wouldest not have made anything if thou hadst hated it. How would anything have endured if thou hadst not willed it? Or how would anything not called forth by thee have been preserved?   *Wisdom 11 : 24–25*

Creator of good
In the beginning God created the heavens and the earth. . . . God created man in his own image . . . and God saw everything that he had made, and behold, it was very good.
     Genesis 1 : 1, 27, 31

Unceasing Sustainer
The Lord is the everlasting God, the Creator of the ends of the earth. He does not faint or grow weary.
     Isaiah 40 : 28

OTHER INSIGHTS

For every age
Genesis is a mystic vision of the origin of things, put in the purest and strongest words, intelligible to the child, inspiring to adult genius, clear enough to survive in primitive eras, and deep enough to challenge sophisticated cultures.   *Herman Wouk*

Leaps forward
It is surely quite clear that if anyone studied the world before there was life on it he could never have predicted life; if he had studied vegetation he would never have predicted animal life; if he had studied the selfishness of mankind he could never have predicted a life of perfect and selfless love. At each stage we reasonably trace the special activity of the will whose purpose is the explanation of all things.   *William Temple*

He made all thing; he loveth it; he keepeth it.
                    Mother Julian of Norwich

The first dawn chorus
G. K. Chesterton, commenting on the verse in the book of Job which speaks of the morning stars singing together and all the sons of God shouting for joy at the act of creation, says, 'One cannot help feeling, even upon this meagre information, that they must have had something to shout about.'

PRAYERS

Blessing the Creator
O Almighty God, without beginning and without end, the Lord of thine own works: we praise and bless thee that thou gavest a beginning to time, and to the world in time, and to mankind in the world; and we beseech thee so to dispose all men and all things that they may be gathered up in thee and thine endless heaven; through him who is the first and the last, thine everlasting Word, our Saviour Jesus Christ.
                    Daily Prayer

The first author of beauty
Lead us, O God, from the sight of the lovely things of the world to the thought of thee their Creator; and grant that delighting in the beautiful things of thy creation we may delight in thee, the first author of beauty and the Sovereign Lord of all thy works, blessed for evermore.

Exploring further

O Lord God, we thank thee that thy Spirit is ever urging the spirits of men to higher achievements of wisdom, skill, love, and goodness. We praise thee for the developing universe, by obeying whose laws men can circle the earth and reach towards the stars. Grant thy wisdom and protection to those who would go still further, and help them to know that they can never overtake thee nor pass out of thy care, through thy perfect Son, Jesus Christ, our Lord.

Fashioning hands

Grant, O my God, that I may keep myself under your loving hands, so that you may complete the work begun in me, and make me more holy, more humble, more loving, more dependent on you, and more serviceable to you, through Jesus Christ, my Saviour.

Blessed be thou, O God, for the loveliness of the created world and for the promise of even greater loveliness in the world to come.

38. GOD IMMANENT

Geologists tell us that the universe has been in existence for 1000 million years or more, and that beginning from lifeless matter, there have been stages of development, each lasting for millions of years. Elements of matter came together to produce new forms. At some stage a cell of life came into being; vegetable life appeared, animal life followed, and finally intelligent man came into being, each new stage being a great leap forward compared with the previous stage. Religious faith sees in this process a divine plan and believes that the initiating purpose is still at work, leading to further development towards the spiritual and the eternal.

INSIGHTS FROM SCRIPTURE

Omnipresent
The Spirit of the Lord has filled the world, and that which holds all things together knows what is said.   *Wisdom 1:7*

Inescapable
Whither shall I go from thy Spirit? Or whither shall I flee from thy presence?   *Psalm 139:7*

No hiding place
Can a man hide himself in secret places so that I cannot see him? says the Lord. Do I not fill heaven and earth?
                                                 Jeremiah 23:24

Near at hand
He is not far from each one of us, for in him we live and move and have our being.   *Acts 17:27–28*

The future anticipated
The kingdom of the world has become the kingdom of our Lord and of his Christ, and he shall reign for ever and ever.   *Revelation 11:15*

OTHER INSIGHTS

God present and active
From the beginning, the Spirit of God has been understood as God in the midst of men, God present and active in the world, God in his closeness to us as a dynamic reality shaping the lives and histories of men. The Spirit, in this sense, is not something other than God, but God in that manner of the divine Being in which he comes closest, dwells with us, acts upon us.   *John Macquarrie*

From glory to glory
A great modern thinker, Teilhard de Chardin, sees the following stages in the work of the Creator Spirit:

> Vitalizing matter
> Humanizing life
> Unifying mankind
> Spiritualizing men
> Christifying men
> Incorporation into the Eternal.

At work with all men
There is no difficulty in finding the movements of the Spirit, because wherever the fruits of the Spirit are, there is he. If you find something going forward which promotes true fellowship, there you know the Holy Spirit is at work, and you may come yourself increasingly under his influence by taking your share there. It may be that those with whom you join are not themselves Christians, and do not recognize the power that is moving them for what it is. Never mind that. You may have the opportunity of helping them to understand it, to their inestimable gain. But if you cannot, do not let that hinder your co-operation; for it still is the work of the Holy Spirit. *William Temple*

PRAYERS

Hidden glory
Glorious Lord Christ: the divine influence secretly diffused and active in the depths of matter, and the dazzling centre where all the innumerable fibres of the manifold meet; power as implacable as the world and as warm as life; you whose forehead is of the whiteness of snow, whose eyes are of fire, and whose feet are brighter than molten gold; you whose hands imprison the stars; you who are the first and the last, the living and the dead and the risen again; you who gather into your exuberant unity every beauty, every affinity, every energy, every mode of existence; it is you to

whom my being cried out with a desire as vast as the universe,
'In truth you are my Lord and my God.'

Teilhard de Chardin

Builders with God

O thou who hast designed this universe and are ever at
work within it to bring it closer to the divine plan, help us
as we look back on its long history to see thy purpose and
the direction pointing to future development. We would be
builders with thee, rejoicing in thy creative wisdom and
eternal patience, and using the inherent powers discovered
by man in dependence on thee, in love of mankind, and
obeying the laws of thy Kingdom of righteousness and love,
O divine Architect, O unceasing Evolver, O over-Ruler of
all.

Continuing work

O Christ, Teacher and Lord, you have taught us that the
Father has always been at work within the universe, in its
natural processes and in the minds, hearts, and consciences
of men. You have assured us that you too are working to
achieve the Father's purposes of love. Work in us and
through us, O Lord, that when the time comes to commend
our spirits to the Father, it may be in the hope that the task
given us has contributed in some small way to the divine
fullness which is his will. And to him we lift our hearts in
blessing and love.

For from him and through him and to him are all things: to
him be glory for ever. Amen.

39. INCARNATION

Once the Creator Spirit became involved in matter and in
developing life, once the spirit of man was created in the
likeness of the divine Spirit, it would seem natural that he
should become fully incarnate in a person, not only to

manifest the divine life but also to be the prototype of human life. The union of the divine and human in Jesus speaks of the hope of man sharing in the divine life.

INSIGHTS FROM SCRIPTURE

Stamped with God's own character

In many and various ways God spoke of old to our fathers by the prophets; but in these last days he has spoken to us by a Son . . . He reflects the glory of God and bears the very stamp of his nature.   *Hebrews 1 : 1–3*

Taking our nature

In the beginning was the Word, and the Word was with God, and the Word was God . . . And the Word became flesh and dwelt among us, full of grace and truth.

John 1 : 1, 14

Living with us

His name shall be called Emmanuel, which means 'God with us'.   *Matthew 1 : 23*

From the heart of God

No one has ever seen God; but God's only Son, he who is nearest to the Father's heart, he has made him known.

John 1 : 18 (NEB)

OTHER INSIGHTS

Personal and homely

A person came, and lived and loved, and did and taught, and died and rose again, and lives on by his power and his spirit for ever within us and amongst us, so unspeakably rich and yet so simple, so sublime and yet so homely, so divinely above us precisely in being so divinely near – that his character and teaching require, for an ever fuller yet never complete understanding, the varying study, and different experiments and applications, embodiments and unrollings of all the races and civilizations, of all the individual and corporate, the simultaneous and successive experiences of the human race to the end of time.

Friedrich von Hügel

God was in Christ
This Word, this Logos, which Greeks and Hebrews unite in recognizing as the controlling power of the whole universe, is no longer unknown or dimly apprehended. The Light which in some measure lightens every man has shone in its full splendour.

William Temple

Embodied witness
There is only one way of being faithful to the Incarnation, and that is to become an embodied testimony to the living God. Perhaps the core of the apologetic task in every age is to be created in lives rather than in arguments.

Gabriel Marcel

PRAYERS

The unapproachable comes near
Honour and power eternal be to thee, O God: King of kings and Lord of lords, who alone hast immortality, dwelling in light unapproachable, whom no man has seen, nor can see; and to thine only begotten Son, who for us men and for our salvation came down from heaven, and was made man, and through his death and resurrection brought us life and immortality.

New Every Morning (BBC)

Fully human
O Christ, my Lord, you came from God into our life and lived in our world, sharing our nature, subject to the happenings of life and the actions of the people among whom you lived. You went to God, so you are always with God in his presence with us. You are the everliving one, still showing us man as he is meant to be, and sharing with us the results of your victorious life, to enable us to grow into

your likeness. O brother man, O divine Son, O beloved
Lord.

A great and mighty wonder
Lord, let me kneel before thy miracle, – an infant in a
stable on a human mother's breast, from all eternity thine
only begotten Son, thy word from before beginning, God of
God, Light of Light, Very God of Very God, of his own
choice, of thine own purpose, made mortal man . . . O
Christ, let me kneel before the wonder of thy glory thus
made manifest to all flesh.   *Eric Milner-White*

Blessed be thou, O God, who in Jesus Christ didst show
forth thy nature, thy love and thy glory. Blessed for ever.

40. INDWELLING

The Incarnation was not an isolated event, wonderful
though it would have been if it was that and nothing more.
It was the beginning of something new, perhaps rather the
manifestation of something which had never been recognized, but which could now happen in a fully conscious and
effective way. The Spirit of God, incarnate fully and
supremely in Jesus, wishes to indwell every man, not only
as an immanent force, but as an invited, personal guest.

INSIGHTS FROM SCRIPTURE

Extending the Incarnation
Behold, I stand at the door and knock; if any man hears
my voice and opens the door, I will come in to him and eat
with him, and he with me.   *Revelation 3 : 20*

God's home in man
If a man loves me, he will keep my word, and my Father
will love him, and we will come to him and make our home
with him.   *John 14 : 23*

An organic unity
Abide in me, and I in you. As the branch cannot bear fruit
by itself, unless it abides in the vine, neither can you, unless
you abide in me.   *John 15:4*

Paul's prayer for his friends
That Christ may dwell in your hearts through faith . . . that
you may be filled with all the fullness of God.
Ephesians 3: 17, 19

OTHER INSIGHTS

The divine presence
Life in the Spirit is to be possessed and feel ourselves
possessed by an inward power and presence greater than
ourselves, a power and presence which we acknowledge to
be God working in us, to give us spiritual enlightenment as
to the purpose of life, and the knowledge of himself, and
personal guidance, and power to control our passions, and
the pre-eminent gift of love.   *Charles Gore*

Expectant
> I have a temple, I do not
> Visit, a heart I have forgot,
> A self that I have never met,
> A secret shrine – and yet, and yet
>
> This sanctuary of my soul
> Unwitting I keep white and whole
> Unlatched and lit, if thou should'st care
> To enter or to tarry there.   *C. H. Sorley*

Compelling priority
Creative power, a torrent of life, fire which burns away
dross, blazing objective truth in which our little opinions
shrivel and vanish, a compelling presence which strengthens
men to heroic action and shapes their mouths to inspired
utterance. The Creator Spirit will be no man's after-

thought. If we seek his help it must be as leader, pilot, inspirer and initiator of all that is to be done. The creative energy of God has absolute priority.   *Ruth Henrich*

PRAYERS .

Look within

Too late I loved thee, O Beauty of ancient days, yet ever new! Thou wast within and I abroad searching for thee! Thou wert with me, but I was not with thee.

St Augustine

God in Christ

O Christ, my Lord, you came from the Father, you lived among men and showed them the Father, you went to the Father, you are ever omnipresent with him. In the depths of our being tell us about the Father and send us to him so that we may know our Creator, our Father and your Father, your God and our God, ever-loving and ever-loved, ever-blessing and ever-blessed, to whom be all the love of our hearts and the devotion of our worship, now and always.

Christ within

O Christ, I believe that I am made in the image of God, akin to him and to you. You are the full and true likeness of God. Come, O Christ, in all your fullness to live within me, and develop the embryo divine likeness to its full maturity. Make me conscious of your presence, responsive to it and grateful for it, O Christ from God, O Christ within.

On the latch

Jesus, Lord, for whom an inn could find no room, whom thine own world would not receive, never let me close my door against thee, nor against the least of my brethren in their least need.

Stand not then at my door and knock, though that be

a miracle of mercy, but lift the latch and enter, Jesus, Lord.
Eric Milner-White

O my soul, today salvation has come to our house.
Bless the Lord, O my soul.

41. TRANSCENDENT

Many people today find it difficult to believe in a personal and transcendent God. Others seem ready to believe in a spirit working within the being of man, almost deifying a kind of common religious consciousness. The three great monotheistic religions confess faith in a transcendent God, basing their belief on the spiritual experience of their founders, prophets and saints and their own religious experience.

INSIGHTS FROM SCRIPTURE

Eternally the same
Thou, Lord, didst found the earth in the beginning, and the heavens are the work of thy hands; they will perish, but thou remainest; they will all grow old . . . But thou art the same, and thy years will never end.   *Hebrews 1:10–12*

Highest and holiest
For thus says the high and lofty One who inhabits eternity, whose name is Holy: I dwell in the high and holy place, and also with him who is of a contrite and humble spirit.
Isaiah 57:15

Infinitely higher
For my thoughts are not your thoughts, neither are your ways my ways . . . For as the heavens are higher than the earth, so are my ways higher than your ways and my thoughts than your thoughts.   *Isaiah 55:8–9*

The worship of heaven
Blessing and glory and wisdom and thanksgiving and
honour and power and might be unto our God for ever and
ever.   *Revelation 7:12*

OTHER INSIGHTS

The otherness of God
In so far as God and man are spiritual they are of one kind;
in so far as God and man are rational, they are of one kind.
But in so far as God creates, redeems and sanctifies while
man is created, redeemed and sanctified, they are of two
kinds. God is not creature; man is not creator. God is not
redeemed sinner, man is not redeemer from sin. At this
point the Otherness is complete.   *William Temple*

Partners in witness
If there is anything which this age demands, if there is
anything that gives reason for hope, it is this: Christian and
Jew, each within the common religious dialogue and also
independent of it, each faithful to his own beliefs and his
own way of life, bear common witness together before the
world that they possess tidings from the divine realm: they
go through history together as corporeal evidence of the
truth of God.   *Schoeps*

At the end
> There in that other world, what waits for me?
> What shall I find after that new birth?
> No stormy, tossing, frowning, smiling sea,
>   But a new earth.
>
> No sun to mark the changing of the days,
> No slow, soft falling of the alternate night,
> No morn, no stars, no light upon my ways,
>   Only the light.

No gray cathedral, wide and wondrous fair,
That I may tread where all my fathers trod.
Nay, nay, my soul, no house of God is there,
   But only God!   *Mary Coleridge*

PRAYERS

Origin and Goal

O God, I see signs of thy presence in every activity of men, expressions of beauty in the arts of men, principles of truth in the sciences of men, marks of nobility in ordinary lives.

O God, I see signs of thy presence in every place, in every bush, in every creature.

Thou art indeed the fount of truth, the first author of beauty, the source of love, the creator and father of all, from all eternity to all eternity, ever the unchanging self from whom our lesser selves derive, in whom they find their source and goal.

Glory be to thee O God eternal.

Partners in worship

O God, I thank thee for Muhammad and for his Muslim followers who assert thy transcendence, thy sovereignty and thy unity. Grant that Christians and Muslims may speak to each other from their experience of thee, that thine 'allness' may be clear to both, and that together we may prostrate ourselves before thy majesty and worship thee as the Sovereign Lord of all.

With all our being

Eternal Light, shine into our hearts,
Eternal Goodness, deliver us from evil,
Eternal Power, be our support,
Eternal Wisdom, scatter the darkness of our ignorance,
Eternal Pity, have mercy upon us; that with all our heart and mind and soul and strength we may seek thy face and be brought by thine infinite mercy to thy holy presence; through Jesus Christ our Lord.   *Alcuin*

Thine, O Lord, is the greatness,
and the power, and the glory,
and the victory, and the majesty;
for all that is in the heavens
and in the earth is thine;
thine is the kingdom, O Lord,
and thou art exalted as head above all.

1 Chronicles 29 : 11

42. PERMEATING

Many religious people are troubled about the secularization of modern life. In one way this is good and right, for values which were once thought of as religious have now passed into the texture of society. Also there are areas of human life which have their own distinctive laws which ought not to be governed by religious views or ecclesiastical direction. On the other hand, Christians must question the assumption that man's relation to the objective world is the whole of life. There is a spiritual dimension of life which people ignore at their peril. The aim for the Christian is to humanize the sacred and to regard the whole of life as good and God-given.

INSIGHTS FROM SCRIPTURE

Hidden permeation
The kingdom of heaven is like leaven which a woman took and hid in three measures of flour, till it was all leavened.

Matthew 13 : 33

Hidden guardians
So the Lord opened the eyes of the young man, and he saw; and behold, the mountain was full of horses and chariots of fire round about Elisha.

2 Kings 6 : 17

A presence felt
Surely the Lord is in this place; and I did not know it.
Genesis 28 : 16

A presence unrecognized
He was in the world, and the world was made through him,
yet the world knew him not.   *John 1 : 10*

Sacred symbols no longer needed
And I saw no temple in the city, for its temple is the Lord
God the Almighty and the Lamb.   *Revelation 21 : 22*

OTHER INSIGHTS

Religionless?
I often ask myself why a Christian instinct frequently draws
me more to the religionless than to the religious, by which I
mean not with any intention of evangelizing them, but
rather, I might almost say, in 'brotherhood'. While I often
shrink with religious people from speaking of God by name –
because that name somehow seems to me here not to ring
true, and I strike myself as rather dishonest (it is especially
bad when others start talking in religious jargon: then I dry
up almost completely, and feel somehow oppressed and ill
at ease) – with people who have no religion I am able on
occasion to speak of God quite openly and as it were
naturally.   *Dietrich Bonhoeffer*

Sacred and secular
It is not only by the way a man speaks of God, but by the
way he speaks of earthly things that one can find out
whether his soul has dwelt in the fire of God's love.
Fr Perron

God is to be sought and honoured in every pursuit and not
merely in something technically called religious.
F. D. Maurice

The task is to humanize the sacred and to sanctify the secular.

Rabbi Abraham Heschel

Mission accomplished

St John saw no temple in his vision of the new Jerusalem. The temple as the symbol of the sacred is no longer needed, because its mission has been accomplished. God is in everything. In one way the eternal city is a secular city; in another way the secular world has been permeated and become sacred.

PRAYERS

Finding life in Christ

By virtue of the Creation and, still more, of the Incarnation, nothing here below is profane for those who know how to see . . . In the life which wells up in me and in the matter which sustains me, I find much more than your gifts. It is you yourself whom I find, you who makes me participate in your Being, you who moulds me. *Teilhard de Chardin*

Permeating human life

Grant, O Lord, that thy Spirit may permeate every sphere of human thought and activity. Let those who believe in thee take with them into their daily work the values of thy Kingdom, the insights of the Gospel and the love of their fellow-men. Hasten the time when justice and brotherhood shall be established and when all men shall be brought into the unity of thy Son, our Saviour Jesus Christ.

Extension of love

Lord, let me rejoice when compassion is no longer a religious virtue, but becomes part of human life. Let me be glad to see goodness in ordinary lives. Let me be thankful as governments take over charitable care from the churches; knowing that the Kingdom of God is becoming in some measure the Kingdom of the world. Let me praise thee, O God, that the more fully human we become, the closer we get to the divine, as seen in the life of him who was true God and full man, even Jesus Christ, thine incarnate Son.

O God, let me rejoice with thee in every sign of truth, beauty, goodness and love, wherever I find them.

VII. WHO IS CHRIST?

This is a question that has been discussed for over nineteen centuries, and people disclose something of their own character by their reaction to it.

43. A VITAL QUESTION

Gospel questionings
What sort of man is this? . . . What do you say about him?
. . . What is this? A new teaching! Even the unclean
spirits . . . obey him . . . Who do men say that the Son of
Man is? . . . Can anything good come out of Nazareth? . . .
Where are you from?
Matthew 8:27, John 9:17, Mark 1:27,
Matthew 16:13, John 1:46, John 19:9

Beginning of faith
He taught them as one who had authority . . . No man ever
spoke like this man . . . I am not worthy to have you come
under my roof; but only say the word . . . I believe; help
my unbelief!   *Matthew 7:29, John 7:46,*
Matthew 8:8, Mark 9:24

Rejection
It is blasphemy! Who can forgive sins but God alone? . . .
You are a Samaritan and have a demon . . . Away with
him, crucify him!   *Mark 2:7, John 8:48, John 19:15*

Acceptance
Lord, to whom shall we go? You have the words of eternal
life . . . You are the Christ, the Son of the living God . . . My
Lord and my God! . . . Who are you, Lord?
John 6:68, Matthew 16:16,
John 20:28, Acts 9:5

Jesus in the Koran
A messenger of God . . . God's prophet . . . Messiah . . .
'Not Son of God' . . . Word of God . . . Servant of God . . .
'He did not die, he was not crucified' . . . he ascended to
heaven . . . he will return as Judge.

OTHER INSIGHTS

Only in his fellowship
He comes to us . . . as of old, by the lake-side, he came to those
men who knew him not. He speaks to us the same word:
'Follow thou me!' and sets us to the tasks which he has to
fulfil for our time. He commands. And to those who obey
him . . . he will reveal himself in the toils, the conflicts, the
sufferings which they shall pass through in his fellowship,
and, as an ineffable mystery, they shall learn in their own
experience who he is.   *Albert Schweitzer*

Not the usual categories
From my youth onwards I have found in Jesus my great
brother. That Christianity has regarded and does regard
him as God and Saviour has always appeared to me as a
fact of the highest importance which for his sake and my
own I must endeavour to understand . . . My own frater-
nally open relationship to him has grown even stronger and
dearer, and today I see him more strongly and clearly than
ever before.

I am more than ever certain that a great place belongs
to him in Israel's history of faith and that this place cannot
be described by any of the usual categories.   *Martin Buber*

A steadying principle
There are times when we can never meet the future with
sufficient elasticity of mind, especially if we are locked in
the contemporary systems of thought. We can do worse
than remember a principle which both gives us a firm
Rock and leaves us the maximum elasticity for our minds:
the principle: Hold to Christ, and for the rest be totally
uncommitted.   *Herbert Butterfield*

For all
I believe that he belongs not only to Christianity but to the
entire world, to all races and people; it matters little under

what flag, name, or doctrine they may work, profess a faith, or worship a God inherited from the ancestors.

Mahatma Gandhi

PRAYERS

Gratitude for Jesus
O Lord God, I have learned more of truth from Jesus Christ than from anyone else. In the fallible records of his life I have seen truth, and in meditating upon them I have found deeper and more personal truth. In his movement within my being I have experienced truth. Thanks be to thee, O God, for Jesus Christ, thy Word and thy Truth.

Following Jesus
O God, let me follow Jesus of Nazareth in simplicity and faith. Let him be such a part of my life that my attitudes, my thinking and behaviour may be based on him. May I know him so intimately that I may speak of him naturally and happily. Help me to be his follower – in every part of my life and in every day of my life, for his sake and for my own sake.

Light from Christ
O Lord Christ, ever-living and ever-present, make known to me the ways of God and his purpose in human history. Interpret to me the meaning of your own incarnate life, and the experience of your earliest disciples. Open my eyes to see you working unrecognized with men of goodwill who seek truth and practise the virtue they know. Make relevant to my life and the world in which I live, the truth about yourself. Let me have something of your mind and heart and character, and infuse into me your Spirit to be my light, my life, my love, my strength. O Lord Christ, ever-living, ever-present.

O Christ, you are God speaking, God calling, God loving, God caring, God drawing, God saving. Thanks be to God for you! Thanks be to you for 'God'!

44. REALLY MAN

Faith in Jesus Christ varies in its emphasis from age to age. The emphasis today is on his humanity. Many feel that he can be of little help to us, unless he became really one of us, with our weaknesses, our temptations, our failures and fears, our hopes and efforts. A God in disguise is of little help to us. But a full, true man is. Many are prepared to think out how close perfect humanity comes to divinity.

INSIGHTS FROM SCRIPTURE

Born
She gave birth to her first-born son and wrapped him in swaddling clothes, and laid him in a manger.   *Luke 2:7*

Tired
Jesus, wearied as he was with the journey, sat down beside the well.   *John 4:6*

Of limited knowledge
Of that day or that hour no one knows, not even the angels in heaven, nor the Son, but only the Father. *Mark 13:32*

Tempted
For we have not a high priest which cannot be touched with the feeling of our infirmities; but was in all points tempted like as we are, yet without sin.   *Hebrews 4:15*

Troubled
My soul is very sorrowful, even to death.   *Mark 14:34*

Died
Then Jesus, crying with a loud voice, said, 'Father, into thy hands I commit my spirit!' And having said this he breathed his last.   *Luke 23:46*

Buried
Now in the place where he was crucified there was a garden, and in the garden a new sepulchre, wherein was never man yet laid . . . There laid they Jesus.   *John 19:41–42*

OTHER INSIGHTS

Homely and natural
For six weeks of springtime nineteen centuries ago the perfected Man was seen and lived in the same earth that the unfallen Adam, the germinal man, had walked millions of years before, and that we live in now. At will he showed himself, at will he was unseen. He consorted with his friends, went for walks, and shared a supper, and picnicked by the lake. Nothing could have been homelier, nothing more natural; that is the point. And his sole resurrection from the unnumbered myriads of the dead is the pledge and proof that the road to man's natural perfection once more lies open to all the sons of men.   *CSMV member*

Powers open to all
We must think of the powers exercised by Christ, as being powers open to manhood where manhood is found in its perfection.   *Professor Leonard Hodgson*

Fellow-travellers so far
There are many people who cannot accept the divinity of Jesus, but who accept him as the greatest of men. I can walk a long way with such people, if they are prepared to take him as their human model. Others hail Jesus as the greatest of teachers. I can accompany them quite a way, if they are ready to follow his teaching. At some point I must be ready to go further, alone if necessary.

PRAYERS

Like us: like him

O Lord Jesus Christ, who hast deigned to be made like unto men; the sharer of our sorrows, the companion of our journeys, the light of our ignorance, the remedy of our infirmity: so fill us with thy Spirit, and endue us with thy grace, that as thou hast been made like unto us, we may grow more like unto thee; for thy mercy's sake.

Jeremy Taylor (adapted)

Pattern for inner likeness

Lord of my life, to thee I call,
    Be in my heart today,
And make me think and speak and act
    As thy dear child alway.
The image of thyself in me
    At my creation given,
O let it both mature and grow,
    And fit me for thy heaven.

To help that inner likeness grow
    A pattern thou hast sent.
Jesus thy Son is Son of Man
    True man to represent.
Before my eyes thy glory shown,
    A child may understand;
O let me walk each step with him
    Held firmly by his hand.

Shared natures

Almighty God, who didst wonderfully create man in thine own image, and didst yet more wonderfully restore him: grant we beseech thee, that as thy Son, our Lord Jesus Christ, was made in the likeness of men, so we may be made partakers of the divine nature; through the same thy Son, who with thee and the Holy Ghost liveth and reigneth, one God, world without end. Amen.

Book of Common Prayer 1928

Blessed be thou, O Christ, true Man and true God, who hast opened for us a new and living way into the presence of God, through the veil of thy flesh. *from Hebrews 10 : 20*

45. HIS MIND

Every disciple knows that the aim of his life is to grow like his Lord. To achieve this he will study the earliest records of the divine life lived among men. He will want to get back behind the words to their meaning, behind the actions to the mind and character which inspired those actions. He will be eager to enter into intimate touch with him who promised to be with men and to live within the inmost being of each man. So with the outer study and the inner communion he will come to understand and acquire something of the mind of Christ.

INSIGHTS FROM SCRIPTURE

A new knowledge
(The prophet asks) 'For who has known the mind of the Lord so as to instruct him?'

 (Paul replies) 'But we have the mind of Christ.'

1 Corinthians 2 : 16

The pattern
Have this mind among yourselves, which is yours in Christ Jesus. *Philippians 2 : 5*

His mind will rule ours
We destroy arguments and every proud obstacle to the knowledge of God, and take every thought captive to obey Christ. *2 Corinthians 10 : 5*

In his confidence
No longer do I call you servants, for the servant does not know what his master is doing; but I have called you friends, for all that I have heard from the Father I have made known to you.

John 15:15

OTHER INSIGHTS

As near as we can get
These writings bring back to you the living image of that most holy mind, the very Christ himself speaking, healing, dying, rising, in fact so entirely present, that you would see less of him if you beheld him with your eyes. *Erasmus*

Characteristics
The dominant characteristic of our Lord's mind was harmony: harmony in itself, with God, and with his environment. It was the harmony of a mind unbrokenly God-centred and utterly free from self-preoccupation.

He was never muddled, never worried, never hurried, never on the edge of a breakdown, because his mind was anchored in God.

He was at ease with everyone he met, and gave each his full attention. He was never perturbed by interruptions.

He was in command of every situation – the hungry crowd, the frightened disciples, in the storm, the police and soldiers who came to arrest him, in his interrogation before the Roman governor. *Maisie Spens*

PRAYERS

Christ my Master
<blockquote>
Christ be my beginning, Christ my end,
Christ my way, and Christ my light,
Christ my energy, and Christ my repose,
Christ my teacher and Christ my truth,
Christ my Master and my all-beloved,
   Christ my Life, my Lord, my God.
</blockquote>

Eric Milner-White

The mind of Christ

O Christ, my Lord, let me have your mind, the priority in all your thinking of the Father, the intention to do the things which the Father is always willing, the quiet trust that the final result is in his hand. O Everlasting One, show me how you lived when you were here in the flesh and how you would live in our complex days of pressure and noise and wider community. Give me your mind for life today and tomorrow and all my days.

The face of Jesus Christ

O thou who art utterly separate in being and entirely present in love, attach our minds, hearts and wills to thee. Help us to look with thine eyes and to care with thy heart, to have thy compassion for evil and thy delight in good; to stand in thy uncreated light and to reflect the light from the face of him, who is thy brightness, Jesus Christ, our Lord.

O Christ, my Master and Lord, grant that I may know thee more clearly, love thee more dearly, follow thee more nearly, day by day.   *St Richard of Chichester*

46. THE KINGDOM

The Kingdom of God was the main subject of the early preaching of Jesus. He claimed that in himself the Kingdom had drawn near, was in operation, and he called to men to accept this fact in faith and to change their attitudes, behaviour and world view. Many of his parables dealt with the meaning of the Kingdom, as if he were wanting to ensure that those who could not at first understand would remember one vivid human story, and that one day the penny would drop. He wanted everyone to share the treasure that he had brought.

INSIGHTS FROM SCRIPTURE

The good news
Jesus came . . . preaching the gospel of God, and saying, 'The time is fulfilled, and the kingdom of God is at hand; repent, and believe in the gospel.'   *Mark 1:14–15*

In the realm of spirit
My kingship is not of this world; if my kingship were of this world, my servants would fight.   *John 18:36*

And to be worked out in society
Pray then like this: . . . Thy Kingdom come, thy will be done, in earth as it is in heaven.   *Matthew 6:9–10*

The end is assured
The sovereignty of the world has passed to our Lord and his Christ, and he shall reign for ever and ever!
Revelation 11:15 (NEB)

OTHER INSIGHTS

The pearl of great price
The Kingdom is something within you which has the power of growth like a seed; something that you discover almost accidentally; something that you are searching for, and of whose value you become more confident and excited as the search proceeds, and you discover truer, lovelier things which are constantly being surpassed; something for which you have to give everything you have, no less yet no more, including the earlier finds with which you were once so completely delighted.

Other facets
Power in complete subordination to love – that is something like a definition of the Kingdom of God.   *William Temple*

To be under the rule of God is to be free from lesser loyalties, even if it involves suffering.

The Kingdom of God in the mind of Jesus was a continuation of the Law of the Lord so precious in the minds of his own people.

The King has come

Man cannot meet his own deepest need, nor find for himself release from his profoundest trouble. What he needs is not progress, but redemption. If the Kingdom of God is to come on earth, it must be because God first comes on earth himself. *William Temple*

Salvation today

Today men are more conscious of the need of salvation in this world – freedom from oppression, fear, poverty, hunger, disease, exploitation, regimentation, bureaucracy. These freedoms will come when the spirit of man, in individuals and in solidarities, is freed and redeemed, and ruled by the righteousness and love of God.

PRAYERS

Signs of the dawn

O Lord, who hast set before us thy great hope that thy Kingdom shall come, and hast taught us to pray for its coming: give us grace to discern the signs of its dawning, and to work for the perfect day when thy will shall be done on earth as it is in heaven; through Jesus Christ our Lord. *Percy Dearmer*

Working together

Loving and Holy Spirit of God, we pray:

That we and all men may increasingly work together to establish the kingdom of heaven upon earth;

That the resources of the world may be gathered, distributed and used, with unselfish motives and scientific skill for the greatest benefit of all;

That beauty may be given to our towns, and left to our
countryside;
That children may be finely bred and finely trained;
That there may be open ways, and peace, and freedom,
from end to end of the earth;
And that all men may learn to be lovers through keeping
thy company. In the name of Jesus. Amen.   *G. C. Binyon*

Productiveness
O Creator God, we stand in wonder at the order of harvest
in nature, and we marvel at the promise that there is a
similar order of bounty in the spiritual sphere. Strengthen
us to live in this faith even in the face of failure, partial or
brief success, knowing that in thy ordering there will be
sometimes great success, and in the final consummation of
thy Kingdom complete success.

Blessed be thou, O God, our King! We long for the day
when thou shalt be the one King over all the earth and thy
name one.

47. EVER-PRESENT

In Christian faith Christ is not just a historical figure of
great stature and inspiration who lived in the first thirty
years of the Christian era. He is an ever-present reality. Not
only do we believe that he came from God and that God
was with him and in him, we also believe that he went to
God and is therefore everywhere present with God.

INSIGHTS FROM SCRIPTURE

Present in mission
Lo, I am with you always, to the close of the age.
                                        Matthew 28 : 20

Present in comfort
I will not leave you desolate; I will come to you.

John 14:18

Present in vision
I died, and behold I am alive for evermore.

Revelation 1:18

A new way of knowing
From now onwards, therefore, we do not judge anyone by the standards of the flesh. Even if we did once know Christ in the flesh, that is not how we know him now.

2 Corinthians 5:16 (Jerusalem Bible)

OTHER INSIGHTS

The experience of the living Christ
Mary Magdalen grieving at the garden tomb, the two disciples talking about the happenings of the previous few days or breaking bread together, the eleven cowering in the upper room, the five disciples back at their fishing, all experienced his continuing presence. Later, Stephen at his trial and later as the stones rained down upon him, Paul on the Damascus road and subsequently, John on Patmos, were equally conscious of a presence.

Available today
My spirit can commune with him. His Spirit comes to me. At any moment, in any place, under any circumstance, he can be present, and I can with the speed of thought become conscious of him, talk with him, seek his advice, listen to him, draw on his strength. But the great thing is not that I can go to him, but that he comes to me. His presence is everywhere.

Act of God
His critics and enemies thought that he could be liquidated by killing him. But God was in Christ and men cannot

destroy the power that created and sustains the universe. Instead of an ending, Christ was released by death to become an ever-living power. Death released him to become a universal presence, no longer limited by time and space.

Must be contemporary

> The living truth
> Is what I long to see
> I cannot lean upon
> What used to be
>
> So shut the Bible up
> And show me how
> The Christ you talk about
> Is living now.   *Sydney Carter*

PRAYERS

The serene faith of Christ
Set before our minds and hearts, O heavenly Father, the example of our Lord Jesus Christ, who, when he was upon earth, found his refreshment in doing the will of him that sent him, and in finishing his work. When many are coming and going, and there is little leisure, give us grace to remember him who knew neither impatience of spirit nor confusion of work, but in the midst of all his labours held communion with thee, and even upon earth was still in heaven; where now he reigns with thee and the Holy Spirit, world without end.   *Dean Vaughan*

Peaks and troughs
O Christ, I thank you for moments of vision, when I know that I am held in your love, when I feel you present in the depths of my being, when I see your purpose for the world, when my heart is full of peace and quiet joy. Keep me reminded, O Christ, of these moments of blessing in times of ordinary duty or coldness, so that I may be ready to welcome you again when the eyes of my spirit see through

the clouds that hide you, and I enjoy you more deeply and
gratefully than ever before, O joy of loving hearts, O love
that never tires.

An Indian witness

> As the moon and its beams are one,
>   So that I be one with thee,
> This is my prayer to thee, my Lord,
>   This is this beggar's plea.
>
> As words and their meaning are linked,
>   Serving one purpose each,
> Be thou and I so knit, O Lord,
>   And through me breathe thy speech.
>
> Take thou this body, O my Christ,
>   Dwell as its soul within;
> To be an instant separate
>   I count a deadly sin.

Tilak

Blessed be thou, O Living Christ, who didst appear to thy
earliest disciples and hast been present to every generation
of disciples since. Make thy presence known to me also.

48. THE CHRIST-COMMUNITY

The New Testament speaks of the Church as the Body of
Christ, created by him to carry on the mission with which he
had been entrusted by God. It is to be the community which
embodies his Spirit and carries on his loving, serving, saving
work. Anyone who has studied our Lord in the gospels, seen
his influence in individual lives, or had some spiritual
contact with him, should be able to recognize in the Church
the corporate expression of the personal life portrayed in the
gospels or intuitively perceived in prayer and meditation.

INSIGHTS FROM SCRIPTURE

An organic relationship
I am the vine, you are the branches . . . Abide in me, and I
in you.   *John 15 : 5, 4*

For just as the body is one and has many members, and all
the members of the body, though many, are one body, so
it is with Christ . . . Now you are the body of Christ and
individually members of it.   *1 Corinthians 12 : 12, 27*

A God-given unity
There is one body and one Spirit, just as you were called to
the one hope that belongs to your call, one Lord, one faith,
one baptism, one God and Father of us all, who is above all
and through all and in all.   *Ephesians 4 : 4–6*

A God-given mission
As the Father has sent me, even so I send you . . . Go therefore and make disciples of all nations . . . You shall be my
witnesses in Jerusalem and in all Judea and Samaria and to
the end of the earth.   *John 20 : 21, Matthew 28 : 19,
Acts 1 : 8*

OTHER INSIGHTS

Community of the Spirit
The Church is the community of the Spirit, not as having
a monopoly of the Spirit, but as having been called into
existence by God and entrusted with the word and the
sacraments. In the Church there should be going on in a
concentrated way the work of the Spirit, which in a diffuse
way is going on throughout creation. When the Church is
truly the Church it is introducing a new dimension into the
social situation, thus giving hope for an eventual transformation.

The temptation of the Church

The danger of the Church is always the danger which our Lord met in the Temptation – to try and attain her end by self-preservation, to preserve her life at all costs, to regard herself as a beleaguered fortress, to defend herself against the world, to keep the institution going at all costs, to persuade men not that she will support them, but that they must support her.   *Bishop Robin,* formerly of Adelaide

Constant renewal essential

We can alter ecclesiastical structures, recast our institutions, direct ourselves towards new goals, brush up our theology, scrap our liturgy and use a different one, but none of it is going to lead us to renewal, unless we acquire simplicity of heart.   *Hubert van Zeller*

PRAYERS

Credal marks

O Lord of the Church
  Make the Church one and heal our divisions
  Make the Church holy in all her members and in all her
    branches
  Make the Church catholic, for all men and in all truth
  Make the Church apostolic with the faith and dynamic of
    the first apostles
O Lord of the Church.

Passion for the Kingdom

Spirit of promise, Spirit of unity, we thank thee that thou art also the Spirit of renewal. Renew in the whole Church, we pray thee, that passionate desire for the coming of thy Kingdom which will unite all Christians in one mission to the world. May we grow up together into him who is our head, the Saviour of the world, and our only Lord and Master.

The Christ-Community

O Lord, let the Church be truly your collective body in the world today, the Christ-Community directed by you its head, infused with your Spirit, loving and serving men as you did when you lived our human life. Help the Church to give itself for the world, so that men may have the priceless treasure of your grace and love, O Lord of the Church, O Saviour of the world.

Blessed be thou, O God, who out of love for the world didst send thy Son; blessed be thou, O Christ, who didst so love the world that thou didst create thy Church!

49. OMEGA POINT

We are familiar with the thought of Christ as the fulfilment of the developing hopes of the Old Testament. We have seen his disciples spreading out all over the earth. We have seen the divided Churches coming together towards unity. We have seen his teaching moving from the individual to the corporate sphere. We are now witnessing an inter-faith convergence in which he is the most provocative figure. Paul and John think of him as the animating force, the evolver of the universe and the centre which draws all men into his love and all things into his unity.

INSIGHTS FROM SCRIPTURE

The eternal plan

He has let us know the mystery of his purpose, the hidden plan he so kindly made in Christ from the beginning to act upon when the times had run their course to the end: that he would bring everything together under Christ, as head, everything in the heavens and in the earth.

Ephesians 1 : 9–10
(Jerusalem Bible)

God wanted all perfection to be found in him and all things
to be reconciled through him and for him.

Colossians 1:19–20
(Jerusalem Bible)

Across all human differentiation
You have put on a new self which will progress towards new
knowledge the more it is renewed in the image of its creator;
and in that image there is no room for distinction between
Greek and Jew, between the circumcised and the un-
circumcised, or between barbarian and Scythian, slave and
free man. There is only Christ: he is everything and he is in
everything.

Colossians 3:10–11
(Jerusalem Bible)

Fulfilment of religion
Think not that I have come to abolish the law and the
prophets; I have come not to abolish them but to fulfil
them.

Matthew 5:17

A new solidarity of life
As in Adam all die, so also in Christ shall all be made alive.

1 Corinthians 15:22

OTHER INSIGHTS

The movement of history
The writer of the book of Daniel thinking over the sufferings
of his people under successive empires, sees a vision of four
great beasts coming up out of the sea and later a vision of a
ruler like a son of man to whom all authority is given by the
Most High. His faith is that the final Kingdom will not be
like the Gentile empires, a supremacy of brute force, but a
supremacy humane and spiritual.

Convergence towards a whole
A great Christian thinker, Teilhard de Chardin thanked

God that the earth was round. He saw in the fact, the hope that man's thought and psycho-social energy would not just move indefinitely outwards thinly spread, but would converge. 'Like the meridians as they approached the poles, science, philosophy and religion are bound to converge as they draw nearer to the whole.' Teilhard de Chardin called the point of convergence 'omega', and in a leap of faith identified it with Christ.

Convergence of religions

In his thought and teaching Jesus raises and answers the questions which religious men in every generation ask – the existence of God, the nature of God, the beginning and end of the world process, the meaning and destiny of man, the nature of the good life, what happens after death, how men can deal with their own weakness and sinfulness, and his own place in this. So he is relevant to all religions.

PRAYERS

Open my eyes

Open my eyes, O Lord, that I may see the chariots of fire, the crowd of watching angels and saints, the four living creatures of creation, the hosts of the redeemed, from every nation and every generation, and thyself, standing in the place of power, directing thy kingdom and strengthening every struggling follower. So seeing thee, may I be held quiet and unafraid, ready and daring, to be and to do and to experience all that thy loving wisdom allows or wills, O beloved author and finisher of my faith.

Overcoming divisive factors

God of all nations, we pray thee for all the people of thy earth; for those who are consumed in mutual hatred and bitterness; for those who make war upon their neighbours; for those who tyrannously oppress; for those who groan under cruelty and subjection.

We beseech thee to teach mankind to live together in peace; no man exploiting the weak, no man hating the strong, each race working out its own destiny, unfettered, self-respecting, fearless.

Teach us to be worthy of freedom, free from social wrong, free from individual oppression and contempt, pure of heart and hand, despising none, defrauding none, giving to all men – in all dealings of life – the honour we owe to those who are thy children, whatever their colour, their race or their caste. *J. S. Hoyland*

The Kingdom of God draws near
O Christ, thou hast bidden us pray for the coming of thy Father's Kingdom of truth, righteousness, freedom and love. We thank thee for the inspired souls of all ages who saw afar the shining city of God and gave their lives to follow the vision. We rejoice that today the hope of these pioneers is becoming the faith of millions. As we have mastered nature to gain wealth and power, help us now to master the social relations of mankind, that we may gain justice and a world of brothers. Enable us to make the welfare of all the supreme law of our relationships, so that thy Kingdom may come nearer and thy will be done more effectively, for in thee both were so perfectly embodied, O divine Son, O human brother.

Blessed be thou, O Christ, eternally and persistently at work to draw all things and all processes into the wholeness of the Creator's will, and all men into the unity of the Father's love.

VIII. THROUGH JESUS CHRIST

*What are the benefits Christians believe they receive as a
result of their commitment to Jesus Christ?*

50. THE LOVE OF THE CROSS

When we consider what a high proportion of each of the four gospels is devoted to the Passion, we can estimate the importance they attach to the cross of Jesus. For Jesus himself it is the crucial time, 'the hour has come', and it is to be the hour of glory when God's love will be shown to the uttermost, for no love can be greater than that which is willing to die for a cause and for the people for whom the cause exists. The cross is central to St Paul's thought also, and the writer of the book of Revelation talks of the worship offered to 'the Lamb who was slain' and 'to him who sits upon the throne'.

INSIGHTS FROM SCRIPTURE

The meaning of the cross
God was in Christ, reconciling the world unto himself.
2 Corinthians 5 : 19

The meaning brought home
God shows his love for us in that while we were yet sinners Christ died for us.
Romans 5 : 8

The meaning becomes personal
I have been crucified with Christ; it is no longer I who live, but Christ who lives in me; and the life I now live in the flesh I live by faith in the Son of God, who loved me and gave himself for me.
Galatians 2 : 20

The cross is essential
Anyone who wishes to be a follower of mine must leave self behind; he must take up his cross, and come with me.
Mark 8 : 34 (NEB)

OTHER INSIGHTS

God in Christ

Since the Friday which we now call 'Good', Christians have interpreted the cross in different ways. At one time some thought of it as the sacrifice of a loving Saviour to a righteous and angry God. Others have thought of it as a ransom paid to the devil. The most vital thought is that of St Paul – God-was-in-Christ. There was identity of mind, heart and purpose, when once again God must have declared 'Thou art my beloved Son, in whom I am well pleased.' The cross inflicted by men was taken over by God and made the manifestation of love and the instrument of salvation.

The tangent point

When Jesus died on the cross there was for the first time in human history a man completely identified with the will of God. So God's will for him could be done, God's will could be done through him, the love and life of God could have uninterrupted flow through him. Jesus is the point where the life of God touches the life of men.

A turning point

With the insight of a prophet and the skill of an artist the writer of the first gospel describes a series of symbolic events connected with the death of Christ. The sun veils its face in shame for the evil which caused the cross. The curtain of the temple is rent, signifying that the way to God is now open to everybody. The earth is shaken and judged and is no longer the cave of death. The dead are raised because one man has committed his spirit into his Father's hands. Nature has received another meaning; history is transformed; you and I are no longer what we were before.

Paul Tillich (summarized)

PRAYERS

A thanksgiving

Blessed be thy name, O Jesu, Son of the most high God; blessed be the sorrow thou sufferedst when thy holy hands and feet were nailed to the tree; and blessed thy love when, the fullness of pain accomplished, thou didst give thy soul into the hands of the Father; so by thy Cross and precious Blood redeeming all the world, all longing souls departed and the numberless unborn; who now livest and reignest in the glory of the eternal Trinity, God for ever and ever.

Eric Milner-White

Entering into Christ's experience

O Christ, whose wondrous birth meaneth nothing unless we be born again, whose death and sacrifice nothing unless we die unto sin, whose resurrection nothing if thou be risen alone: raise and exalt us, O Saviour, both now to the estate of grace and hereafter to the state of glory; where with the Father and the Holy Spirit thou livest and reignest, God for ever and ever.

Daily Prayer

The true cross

O Saviour Lord, crucified for me, crucified by me, attach me to the long line of pilgrims who have sought and discovered the true cross:

not the old worn wood, but its living grace;

not the cruel relic of a bygone woe, but the wisdom of God for the mind, the power of God for the will, the patience of God towards our angers and ignorances, thy generosity unto death.

Eric Milner-White

Worthy is the Lamb who was slain, to receive power and wealth and wisdom and might and honour and glory and blessing! . . . To him who sits upon the throne and to the Lamb be blessing and honour and glory and might for ever and ever!

Revelation 5: 12, 13

51. REDEMPTION THROUGH THE CROSS

We Christians often use the words 'Christ died to save us from our sins.' He shows us the limitless measure of God's love and that draws our hearts to him. He makes known to us God's forgiveness, not only in his teaching, but by the fact of his own forgiveness of those who brought him to the cross. There is something more which it is difficult to describe – he works within us, assuring us of God's forgiveness, changing our hearts towards sin and selfishness, and sharing his risen life so that sin, though it may attack us, need find no entry.

INSIGHTS FROM SCRIPTURE

Conditions of redemptive vocation
Therefore I will divide him a portion with the great, and he shall divide the spoil with the strong; because he poured out his soul to death, and was numbered with the transgressors; yet he bore the sin of many, and made intercession for the transgressors.   *Isaiah 53 : 12*

The condition of spiritual harvest
Truly, truly, I say to you, unless a grain of wheat falls into the earth and dies, it remains alone; but if it dies, it bears much fruit.   *John 12 : 24*

The drawing power of the cross and the ascension
I, when I am lifted up from the earth, will draw all men to myself.   *John 12 : 32*

The cost of redemption
You were ransomed from the futile ways inherited from your fathers, not with perishable things such as silver or gold, but with the precious blood of Christ, like that of a lamb without blemish or spot.   *1 Peter 1 : 18–19*

OTHER INSIGHTS

Undeserving but accepted
Justification is the establishment of a permanent relationship between a gracious God and those who are desperately in need of his grace. It is that act in which God declares himself to be unalterably favourable to one who is totally undeserving of his favour. It is that act in which a man who knows himself to be a sinner abandons every claim on God and every attempt to establish his own righteousness, and declares his intention to rest for ever and only on the forgiveness of God declared and made real to him in Jesus Christ. *Stephen Neill* in an
unpublished manuscript

The redemptive force of love
For the creative Charity of God, as experienced by man, is a redemptive force. It comes into human life in Christ, his Spirit, his Church, his sacraments, and his saints, not to inform but to transform; to rescue from the downward pull which is felt throughout the natural order, to reform, energize, and at last sanctify the souls of men, making those rescued souls in their turn part of the redeeming organism through which the salvation of the world shall be achieved.
Evelyn Underhill

Continuing redemption
No baseness or cruelty of treason so deep or so tragic shall enter our human world, that the loyal love shall be able in due time to oppose to just that deed of treason its fitting deed of atonement. The deed of atonement shall be so wise and so rich in its efficacy that the spiritual world, after the atoning deed, shall be better, richer, more triumphant amid all its irrevocable tragedies, than it was before the traitor's deed was done. *Josiah Royce*

PRAYERS

Without Jesus Christ

O Lord Jesus Christ, without you I would not have known the limitless love of God. Without you I would not have known the extent of God's forgiveness or seen it in operation on the cross. Without your rescue I would still be submerged in weakness and sin. Without you I would not have the divine grace to transform my life. Without you I would not have known of the Kingdom of God or our Father's plan to unite humanity in righteousness and love. I can never thank you enough, or love you enough, my Redeemer and the Saviour of the world.

Mindful of the love

Lord God, in return for thy great love I would bring an offering, but there is only one worthy offering, the perfect obedience of thy Son even unto death.

Lord God, I remember that offering, I plead it before thee.

And though it be all-sufficient I add to it the offering of myself, body, mind, and spirit, mind, heart, and will, all that I have, all that I am, all that by thy grace I can become.

Accept, O Lord God, this unworthy sacrifice and cleanse and sanctify and use it in the service of thy Kingdom for his dear sake.

Crucified with Christ

O God our Father, help us to nail to the cross of thy dear Son the whole body of our death, the wrong desires of the heart, the sinful devisings of the mind, the corrupt apprehensions of the eyes, the cruel words of the tongue, the ill employment of hands and feet; that the old man being crucified and done away, the new man may live and grow into the glorious likeness of the same thy Son Jesus Christ;

who liveth and reigneth with thee and the Holy Ghost, one God, world without end. *Eric Milner-White*

Blessed be thou, O Lord Christ, who didst die not to save us from punishment, but to save us from our sins and to raise us to new life.

52. LIBERATION THROUGH CHRIST

Freedom in Christ is not freedom to do what I like, but freedom to be what I am meant to be. It is freedom from all the chains which hold me back from being my true self. It is freedom from all imposed limitations and external pressures. It is to share in Christ's freedom to do God's will, and then to help others find a similar freedom.

INSIGHTS FROM SCRIPTURE

The Spirit of the Lord God is upon me, because the Lord has anointed me to bring good tidings to the afflicted; he has sent me to bind up the broken-hearted, to proclaim liberty to the captives, and the opening of the prison to those who are bound. *Isaiah 61:1*

Today this scripture has been fulfilled in your hearing.
Luke 4:21

If the Son makes you free, you will be free indeed.
John 8:36

Now the Lord is the Spirit, and where the Spirit of the Lord is, there is freedom. *2 Corinthians 3:17*

The perfect law, the law of liberty. *James 1:25*

OTHER INSIGHTS

Inner freedom or outer compulsion

To be raised from the dead is to be no longer the prisoner of one's environment. It is to be free from the chains of one's conditioning. It is to realize that it is not necessary to play the game which is being played on us, so that we can play our own game not the one imposed. That is the secret so far unlearnt by those who despitefully use us. They react to life as life has treated them. They are bloody because life is bloody . . . let us be free to be our own master and to live our own life, and not to be merely the sport and toy of circumstance, with everything we do automatically dictated by what is done to us.   *H. A. Williams*

Glorious liberty

When a man is true, if he were in hell he could not be miserable. He is right with himself because right with him whence he came. To be right with God is to be right with the universe: one with the power, the love, the will of the mighty Father, the cherisher of joy, the Lord of laughter, whose are all glories, all hopes, who loves everything and hates nothing but selfishness.   *George Macdonald*

The freedoms of faith

Faith enables us to get free from –

1. The domination of place and time, for it gives the additional dimension of the spiritual and the eternal.

2. The domination of happenings, for we are not at the mercy of circumstances, but can draw upon the inexhaustible wisdom and grace of God.

3. The domination of the written word, for we do not identify it with the inerrant word of God, but test it by the incarnate word.

4. The domination of theology, for men's thoughts about God change, and our theories, however good, are seen to be imperfect.

5. The domination of puritanism, for we see that truth and love must be decisive about action.

6. The domination of conscience, for conscience constantly needs educating from our growing knowledge of God.

PRAYERS

Freedom through obedience

O thou who hast taught us that we are most truly free when we lose our wills in thine: help us to attain to this liberty by continual surrender unto thee; that walking in the way which thou hast prepared for us, we may find our life in doing thy will; through Jesus Christ our Lord.

Gelasian Sacramentary

Freedom of the Spirit

O Holy Spirit, whose presence is liberty, grant us that freedom of the Spirit, which will not fear to tread in unknown ways, nor be held back by misgivings of ourselves or fear of others. Ever beckon us forward to the place of thy will which is also the place of thy power, O ever-leading, ever-loving Lord.

Freedom from lesser loyalties

O God, I know that if I do not love thee with all my heart, with all my mind, with all my soul and with all my strength, I shall love something else with all my heart and mind and soul and strength. Grant that putting thee first in all my lovings I may be liberated from all lesser loves and loyalties, and have thee as my first love, my chiefest good and my final joy.

Blessed be thou, O Lord Christ, who hast set me free to be true to the divine likeness which thou hast implanted in me.

53. JESUS THE HEALER

The healing acts of Jesus are acted parables telling us that God's will is health and healing: the blind receive their sight, the deaf hear and the dumb speak, cripples walk, those with infectious diseases are cleansed, the mentally and spiritually sick are helped to overcome feelings of guilt, paralysing fears, failures to face the responsibilities of life, inner divisions. The gospels give us the impression that the sick were healed with a word – perhaps it was a relevant word that had to go home to the heart, be accepted and implemented in faith.

INSIGHTS FROM SCRIPTURE

The healing of Jesus
He went about all Galilee, teaching in their synagogues and preaching the gospel of the kingdom and healing every disease and every infirmity among the people.

Matthew 4:23

The healing mission
And he called to him his twelve disciples and gave them authority over unclean spirits, to cast them out, and to heal every disease and every infirmity.

Matthew 10:1

The healing community
Is any among you sick? Let him call for the elders of the church, and let them pray over him, anointing him with oil in the name of the Lord; and the prayer of faith will save the sick man, and the Lord will raise him up; and if he has committed sins, he will be forgiven.

James 5:14–15

The prayer for healing
So the sisters sent to him, saying, 'Lord, he whom you love is ill.'

John 11:3

OTHER INSIGHTS

Implanted healing
The body has its own techniques for dealing with the threat of disease, and organizes its powers to resist the invading infection or heal the physical injury. The very symptoms of disease are often pressures towards health, and a neurosis may be the healthiest possible solution at the moment for the psychological problems of the mentally sick. The creator has implanted in body and mind the urge towards healing.

Inner healing
The paralysed man (Mark 2 : 1–12) could not get free from a feeling of guilt and was healed by the word of forgiveness. The paralysed man at the Sheep Gate (John 5:2–9) was asked 'Do you want to be healed?' inferring that he preferred to escape from the responsibilities of daily life. The man who called himself Legion (Mark 5:1–20) had his many divisions unified in the acceptance of Christ's authority and encouragement. Many of our troubles are spiritual and will not be healed by treating the physical symptoms but only by tackling the spiritual causes – fear of failure, fear of ridicule, anxiety, frustrated irritation, escapism, inner division, feelings of guilt for which we are not humble enough or wise enough to accept God's forgiveness.

The part of the Church
Any community of Christians will have a concern for all its members. When any member is ill, the others will rally round in sympathy and helpfulness. There will be believing and persistent prayer, calling God's love to the aid of those in trouble, so much greater and more effective than our own. The Church will also be engaged in preventive health, teaching people how to live a disciplined life avoiding over-eating, over-drinking, over-working, a trusting life avoiding anxiety, impatience, frustration, a psychologically healthy life so that they never come to a stage where

psychiatric treatment or a period in a mental hospital is needed. Living in Christ's way will enable us to share in Christ's health, and make available to us the abundant life of spirit, mind and body which is God's will for all.

PRAYERS

For spiritual healing

Almighty God, who calledst Luke the Physician, whose praise is in the Gospel, to be an Evangelist, and Physician of the soul: May it please thee, that, by the wholesome medicines of the doctrine delivered by him, all the diseases of our souls may be healed; through the merits of thy Son Jesus Christ our Lord.   *Book of Common Prayer*

For spiritual health

O Spirit of God who dost speak to spirits created in thine own likeness: penetrate into the depths of our spirits, into the storehouse of memories remembered and forgotten, into the depths of being, the very springs of personality. And cleanse and forgive, making us whole and holy, that we may be thine and live in the new being of Christ our Lord.

To understand suffering

O Lord, we pray thee for all who are weighed down with the mystery of suffering. Reveal thyself to them as the God of love who thyself dost bear all our sufferings. Grant that they may know that suffering borne in fellowship with thee is not waste or frustration, but can be turned to goodness and blessing, something greater than if they had never suffered, through him who on the cross suffered rejection and hatred, loneliness and despair, agonizing pain and physical death, and rose victorious from the dead, conquering and to conquer, even Jesus Christ our Lord.

For all ministers of healing

Bless, O Lord, all who are co-operating in thy will for healing, all doctors, surgeons, nurses, psychiatrists, research workers, those who cook and serve and clean, all who work in preventive health, all administrators, all who study our social life to help us how to live. We thank thee, O Lord of life and health, for this army of healing workers. Praise be to thee and gratitude to them.

A Blessing
May the Father bless them, who created all things in the beginning; may the Son of God heal them; may the Holy Spirit enlighten them, guard their bodies, save their souls, direct their thoughts, and bring them safe to the heavenly country, where Father, Son, and Holy Spirit ever reign, one God blessed for evermore.

54. DISTURBER OF OUR PEACE

From the first days by the shore of Galilee, people have felt attracted to Jesus. As they have gone on in his company they have seen the gap between themselves and him. They have felt his penetrating knowledge of their inmost being and his intention to free them from their own shortcomings and to help them to maturity. The full humanity of Jesus, his limitless love, his demand for perfection, keep us disturbed, until we are ready to go his way and accept his transforming grace.

INSIGHTS FROM SCRIPTURE

Challenge to conscience
If I had not come and spoken to them, they would not have sin; but now they have no excuse for their sin.
John 15:22

Discipleship involves criticism
Do not think that I have come to bring peace on earth; I have not come to bring peace, but a sword. For . . . a man's foes will be those of his own household.
Matthew 10:34,36

A disconcerting reply
'Teacher, bid my brother divide the inheritance with me.'
... 'Man, who made me a judge or divider over you?' ...
'Beware of all covetousness.'   *Luke 12:13–15*

Far above every other love
If any man comes to me and does not hate his own father
and mother and wife and children and brothers and sisters,
yes, and even his own life, he cannot be my disciple.

                                                Luke 14:26

OTHER INSIGHTS

Inexorable love
Nothing is inexorable but love. Love which will yield to
prayer is imperfect and poor. Nor is it then the love that
yields, but its alloy ... For love loves unto purity. Love has
ever in view the absolute loveliness of that which it beholds.
Where loveliness is incomplete, and love cannot love its fill
of loving, it spends itself to make more lovely, that it may
love more; it strives for perfection, even that itself may be
perfected – not in itself, but in the object ... Therefore all
that is not beautiful in the beloved, all that comes between
and is not of love's kind, must be destroyed. And our God is
a consuming fire.   *George Macdonald*

You must be perfect
Christ will never let us go because he loves and values us so
completely. He will never let us down, however great our
need or difficult our circumstances. He will never let us off
until we become what he wants us to be, for he can never
be content with anything second-rate, anything less than
the highest possible with his grace.

No sentimentality or lip-service
On one occasion three would-be disciples came to Jesus
and offered their discipleship with reservations or delays.
He warned them that discipleship involved hardship, with

total, immediate and life-long commitment (Luke 9:57–62). When we begin to follow we shall soon realize that more is needed, and if we are honest enough or rash enough to ask 'What do I still lack?' he will unerringly put his finger on the one thing we are least ready to surrender.

PRAYERS

Disturber of our peace
O Holy Spirit, who dost so deeply disturb our peace: continue, we pray thee, thy probings and promptings, and goad us until we go thy way, to our own greater blessing and deeper peace, in Jesus Christ our Lord.

Rapier point
O Spirit of God, speak to my spirit in thoughts that pierce to the very centre of my being, cutting through all pretence, evasion, misunderstanding, with the rapier of truth, so that I may know, without the need to reason or explain. Strengthen me from such moments to live in truth.

Never enough
Suffer me never to think that I have knowledge enough to need no teaching, wisdom enough to need no correction, talents enough to need no grace, goodness enough to need no progress, humility enough to need no repentance, devotion enough to need no quickening, strength sufficient without thy Spirit; lest, standing still, I fall back for evermore.
                                                    Eric Milner-White

O Christ my Lord, never let me become self-satisfied, never let me go, never despair of me, never abandon me, but continue your goading, sanctifying, life-giving, love-filling work, until I come closer to your hope and your will for me, O Master and Lord.

55. KING OF SAINTS

Saints are people who have had an encounter with God, however they name him, and have had their lives changed as a consequence. This can be seen significantly in the call of the first disciples, their training by Jesus and their sending out to serve the world in witness and love. None of them were men of wisdom by human standards, none of them from the noblest families or in positions of power. But because of their devotion and faithfulness to our Lord they made their contribution to God's purpose of love. This is repeated in every generation by faithful followers who live for Jesus, if necessary die for him and whatever be the manner of their death die in him.

INSIGHTS FROM SCRIPTURE

A great number
After this I looked, and behold, a great multitude which no man could number, from every nation, from all tribes and peoples and tongues, standing before the throne and before the Lamb, clothed in white robes, with palm branches in their hands, and crying out with a loud voice, 'Salvation belongs to our God who sits upon the throne, and to the Lamb!'
Revelation 7 : 9–10

Surrounding us
Therefore, since we are surrounded by so great a cloud of witnesses, let us also lay aside every weight, and sin which clings so closely, and let us run with perseverance the race that is set before us, looking to Jesus the pioneer and perfecter of our faith, who for the joy that was set before him endured the cross, despising the shame, and is seated at the right hand of the throne of God.
Hebrews 12 : 1–2

Saintliness essential
Strive for peace with all men, and for the holiness without which no one will see the Lord. *Hebrews 12:14*

The key to saintliness
Not every one who says to me, 'Lord, Lord,' shall enter the kingdom of heaven, but he who does the will of my Father who is in heaven. *Matthew 7:21*

OTHER INSIGHTS

The way to saintliness
Let us remember that to become saints we have only
to be what God wants us to be,
to do what God wants us to do;
to forget ourselves and never to forget God;
  We need
perfect simplicity with regard to ourselves,
perfect contentment with all that comes our way,
perfect peace of mind in utter self-forgetfulness.
  This becomes easier as we realize the utter greatness and goodness and 'allness' of God. *Archbishop Goodier*

Everyday saints
    They lived not only in ages past,
      There are hundreds of thousands still;
    The world is bright with the joyous saints
      Who love to do Jesus' will.
    You can meet them in school, or in lanes, or at sea,
      In church, or in trains, or in shops, or at tea,
    For the saints of God are just like me,
      And I mean to be one too. *Lesbia Scott*

A wide communion
In the Apostles' Creed Christians confess their faith in a communion of saints, a fellowship of holy, loving people of all generations who have tried to live according to the light they have received. There is a fellowship of saintliness, a

kinship of character and dedication, which is not confined to the Christian religion only, but comprises all who live by the highest they know and are glad to recognize a similar dedication in other people.

PRAYERS

Thanksgiving for the saints

We thank thee, O God, for the saints of all ages; for those who in times of darkness kept the lamp of faith burning; for the great souls who saw visions of larger truth and dared to declare it; for the multitude of quiet and gracious souls whose presence has purified and sanctified the world; and for those known and loved by us, who have passed from this earthly fellowship into the fuller light of life with thee.

A Book of Prayers for Schools

Example and promise

O King, eternal, immortal, invisible, who in the righteousness of thy saints hast given us an example of godly life, and in their blessedness a glorious pledge of the hope of our calling, we beseech thee that, being compassed about with so great a cloud of witnesses, we may run with patience the race that is set before us, and with them receive the crown of glory that fadeth not away; through Jesus Christ our Lord.

Acts of Devotion

Christification

Strengthen, O Lord, the process of Christification within my spirit, by new insights of truth, further impulses to goodness, deeper consciousness of grace, growing maturity within, wider love of my fellow-men, as well as by my willed communion with thee and my experience of thy Spirit at work within mine, so that I may grow to the true humanity seen in Jesus Christ, my Lord.

Epitaph
We have made this memorial to commemorate those who have fought already, and to train those who shall fight hereafter.

Inscription in the Chapel of Modern Martyrs, St Paul's Cathedral

56. IN DEBT TO CHRIST

It is a good thing to sit down from time to time and reflect on what I owe to Christ. Not only the general things like the knowledge of God, and the assurance of forgiveness and grace, but the things personal to myself. What would I have been like without him? What have been the turning points, the peak moments, the painful experiences, when life struck a hard blow? Above all, what can I become under his transforming hands?

INSIGHTS FROM SCRIPTURE

I know this
Apart from me you can do nothing.   *John 15: 5*

And this also
I can do all things in him who strengthens me.
Philippians 4: 13

The way to God is open
The curtain of the temple was torn in two, from top to bottom.   *Matthew 27: 51*

Human divisions surmounted
He . . . has broken down the dividing wall of hostility.
Ephesians 2: 14

Where to look
Behold the man!   *John 19: 5*

J.S.   G

Spoken to me also
My son, your sins are forgiven.   *Mark 2 : 5*

I glimpse this too
When anyone is united to Christ, there is a new world.
                              2 Corinthians 5 : 17 (NEB)

I hear this also
O man of little faith, why did you doubt? *Matthew 14 : 31*

In every happening
It is I; be not afraid.   *Matthew 14 : 27*

I can stay with him
Father, into thy hands.   *Luke 23 : 46*

The meaning of life
Lord, to whom (else) shall we go? You have the words of
eternal life.
                                        John 6 : 68

He comes to me
Behold, I stand at the door and knock; if any one hears my
voice and opens the door, I will come in to him and eat
with him, and he with me.   *Revelation 3 : 20*

OTHER INSIGHTS

All authority
Jesus means something to our world because a mighty
spiritual force streams forth from him and flows through our
time also . . . To me Jesus remains what he was. Not for a
single moment have I had to struggle for my conviction
that in him is the supreme spiritual and religious authority.
                                        Albert Schweitzer

The divine hands
In the life which wells up in me and in the matter which
sustains me, I find much more than your gifts. It is you

yourself whom I find, you who makes me participate in your being, you who moulds me. Truly in the ruling and in the first disciplining of my living strength, in the continually beneficent play of secondary causes, I touch, as near as possible, the two faces of your creative action, and I encounter, and kiss, your two marvellous hands – the one which holds us so firmly that it is merged, in us, with the sources of life, and the other whose embrace is so wide that, at its slightest pressure, all the springs of the universe respond harmoniously together. *Teilhard de Chardin*

PRAYERS

O Christ!
O Christ, image of God, pattern of man, founder of the Kingdom, fulfiller of men's deepest hopes, encourager of true religion, lover of all men without any human differentiations, leader of all true advance, guide to God, gatherer of all into the brotherhood of man under the fatherhood of God, O Christ, meeting point of all men, all truth, all hopes, O Christ.

A faint reflection
O Lord, I have received so much light from thee that there ought to be a little reflection of light to others; I have received so much love from thee that there ought to be a suggestion of gentleness when others meet me. Grant that it may be so, dear Lord.

None other Lamb
    None other Lamb, none other Name,
        None other Hope in heaven or earth or sea,
    None other Hiding-place from guilt and shame,
        None beside Thee.

    My faith burns low, my hope burns low
        Only my heart's desire cries out in me
    By the deep thunder of its want and woe
        Cries out to Thee.

Lord, Thou art Life tho' I be dead,
Love's Fire Thou art, however cold I be;
Nor heaven have I, nor place to lay my head,
Nor home, but Thee.

Christina Georgina Rossetti

Jesu my Lord, I thee adore,
O make me love thee, more and more.

IX. INNER SPACE

The longest journey
Is the journey inwards.
Of him who has chosen his destiny,
Who has started upon his quest
For the source of his being
                    Dag Hammarskjöld
                        Markings

57. COMMUNICATION

We sometimes think that God spoke to men in the past in a more objective, external way than he speaks to us today. He speaks as he has always done, within the heart of man, in direct intuitive communication or through making relevant to us today, words that he spoke to prophets, saints, and thinkers, recorded in Scripture. Above all he speaks through his eternal word, who became man in Jesus our Christ, whose words and teaching as they were remembered and handed down are recorded in the gospels, and who is ever present with men.

INSIGHTS FROM SCRIPTURE

A God who speaks
The word of the Lord came to me, saying . . .
Old Testament (passim)

A king's wistful question
Is there any word from the Lord?   *Jeremiah 37 : 17*

God's eternal word
In the beginning was the Word, and the Word was with God, and the Word was God. And the Word became flesh and dwelt among us, full of grace and truth. *John 1 : 1, 14*

God's supreme word
In many and various ways God spoke of old to our fathers by the prophets; but in these last days he has spoken to us by a Son . . . He reflects the glory of God and bears the very stamp of his nature.   *Hebrews 1 : 1, 3*

Piercing and unmistakable
For the word of God is living and active, sharper than any two-edged sword, piercing to the division of soul and spirit,

of joints and marrow, and discerning the thoughts and
intentions of the heart.   *Hebrews 4 : 12*

OTHER INSIGHTS

The word in the prophet
In his poem 'The Prophet', the poet Pushkin pictures the
coming of a seraph, who raises the eyelids of prophetic
sight, touches his ears, tears out his vain, sinful, base
tongue, and gives him a serpent's fiery fang, cuts out his
quaking heart and puts a coal of living fire in its place, and
finally commands him:

> Arise! O prophet, having seen and heard:
>   Strong in my spirit span
> The universal earth, and make my word
>   Burn in the heart of man.

via Kenneth Cragg

The word generates faith
(Faith) comes by hearing the word of God, not by studying
objectively the records of the past, not even by studying the
Bible. It comes by accepting a gift that contradicts man's
self-chosen ends, not by weighing all the imagined options.
It comes by a leap of the heart in response to God's promise,
not by careful calculation of various future possibilities. It
comes as a total response of the self to God's eschatological
demand, not by surveying actions that seem expedient at the
moment.   *Paul Minear*

The only obstacle
Self-centredness completely vitiates communication – with
either God or man.   . *Hubert van Zeller*

PRAYERS

Past words live again
O Lord, I know that men in past ages have heard thy word,
for it is so true today; it changed their lives and made them

feel part of a great purpose. Grant that I may relate the truth of thy word in the past to life today. I pray thee also to speak to me anew, new things under new conditions, for the sake of him who was the word made flesh and is the eternal word, revealing meaning and truth, even Jesus Christ, my Teacher and my Lord.

The word is always productive

O Divine Sower, who dost sow the seed of thy word in my inner being, where it can germinate and grow and produce a harvest of truth, love and wisdom; let me too be a sower that my words may fall in good ground and through the germ of truth, love and wisdom, contained in them, produce harvest for thy Kingdom, beyond my own hopes and ability, O Lord of the sowing and Lord of the harvest.

The sharp point of truth

O Spirit of God, speak to my spirit in thoughts that pierce to the very centre of my being, cutting through all pretence, evasion, misunderstanding, with the rapier of truth, so that I may know, without the need to reason or explain. Strengthen me from such moments to live in truth.

I wait for the Lord, my soul waits, and in his word I hope; my soul waits for the Lord more than watchmen for the morning, more than watchmen for the morning.

Psalm 130:5–6

58. PRAYER

The word 'prayer' embraces a number of meanings and covers a number of activities. In its most elementary form it is asking God for the things we need, material or spiritual. It can be thanksgiving for what God has done for us; it can be worship of God for what he is. It can be fellowship with God, enjoying our touch with him, quiet reflection in his presence. It can be the expression of our concern for people or for what is happening in the world and in the Church. It can be vocal, when we express ourselves in words, or it can be silent and contemplative, resting in his presence, the sphere of the timeless and the eternal. Prayer is as essential to the inner life as breath is to the body.

INSIGHTS FROM SCRIPTURE

We need training
We do not know how to pray as we ought, but the Spirit himself intercedes for us with sighs too deep for words.

Romans 8:26

Lord, teach us to pray.

Luke 11:1

We need discipline
Have no anxiety about anything, but in everything by prayer and supplication with thanksgiving let your requests be made known to God.

Philippians 4:6

One man's question
What is the Almighty, that we should serve him? And what profit do we get if we pray to him?

Job 21:15

Another man's answer
On the day I called, thou didst answer me, my strength of soul thou didst increase.

Psalm 138:3

OTHER INSIGHTS

Our prayers do not change God's mind, elicit his pity or reverse a sentence . . . they allow God to put into operation (in me and through me) something he has willed all along.

Hubert van Zeller

Intercession is a compassionate encounter with the needs of others in the presence of God.

To Muhammad every time of prayer was an ascension and a new nearness to God. *Hujwiri*, a Muslim writer of the 11th century

Contemplative prayer is the prayer of hunger and thirst, of desire for God, be the desire strong or very feeble. It is the prayer in which the self is not pious but simply itself towards reality and God. It is the prayer in which the images and sophistications both of religion and of irreligion are left behind as a person finds in the depth of himself One whom he desires. Such is the prayer which links Christianity and ordinary life. May it also be the prayer which can reach from the religious to the religionless? *Michael Ramsey*

PRAYERS

My first task
Lord, teach me to pray, to want to pray, to delight to pray.
When I pray, teach me to pray with faith, with hope, with love.
Let me make prayer my first work, my persistent work, my most important work.
Work that I do for you, for others, for the whole world.
Let my prayer be a channel for your love, your grace, your peace for those for whom I pray, and for myself,
O dear and blessed Lord. *Eric Milner-White* (summarized)

The essential task
Look well, O soul, upon thyself lest spiritual ambition should mislead thee to thy essential task to wait in quietness: to knock and persevere in humble faith.
Knock thou in love, nor fail to keep thy place before the door, that when Christ comes and not before, he shall open unto thee the treasures of his love. *Fr Gilbert Shaw*

Two aims of prayer
O Lord, we beseech thee mercifully to receive the prayers

of thy people which call upon thee; and grant that they may both perceive and know what things they ought to do, and also may have grace and power faithfully to fulfil the same; through Jesus Christ our Lord. *Book of Common Prayer*

Blessed be God who will not cast out my prayer, nor turn his mercy from me.

59. SILENCE

An ordinary friendship would not get very deep if one of the two friends did all the talking. There needs to be listening as well as speaking, the response of mind and heart to the other. Sometimes words do not seem to be necessary, each just enjoys being with the other. So in our communion with God, there are times when we pour out our hearts in words; there are times when thoughts are too deep for words, and other times when feeling is too deep for thoughts, when the still silence of love received and given is the highest form of communion.

INSIGHTS FROM SCRIPTURE

Alone with God
Jesus, full of the Holy Spirit, returned from the Jordan, and was led by the Spirit for forty days in the wilderness.
Luke 4:1

A poet's example
For God alone my soul waits in silence. *Psalm 62:1*

A prophet's experience
But the Lord was not in the wind . . . not in the earthquake . . . not in the fire; and after the fire a still small voice (RV margin – a sound of gentle stillness). *1 Kings 19:11–12*

Silence after travail of soul
I am of small account: how can I answer thee?
I lay my hand upon my lips; once I have spoken – never
   again!
twice – but I will not say one other word! . . .
I had heard of thee by hearsay, but now mine eyes have
   seen thee;
so I despise myself, in dust and ashes I repent.

> *Job 40: 4–5, 42: 5–6*
> (Moffatt)

Worried about the headlines?
Be still, and know that I am God.   *Psalm 46: 10*

OTHER INSIGHTS

Emptiness
To be empty of all self-concern; to accept quietly one's own
weaknesses and limitations; to be empty of all striving and
even thinking; to be silent and open, so that God can make
his presence felt, speak within us if he will, though what he
says may not be crystallized in thought or word until some
time later. At such times I become my authentic self, as I
am when the image of God in me is allowed to rise into
quiet, alert consciousness. To be trusting, patient, unhurried, expectant and receptive.

The language of silence
Teach us O God that silent language which says all things.
Teach our souls to remain silent in thy presence: that we
may adore thee in the deeps of our being and await all
things from thee, whilst asking of thee nothing but the
accomplishment of thy will. Teach us to remain quiet under
thine action and produce in our souls that deep and simple
prayer which says nothing and expresses everything, which
specifies nothing and expresses everything.   *J. N. Grou*

Sensing the depths
Lord, the Scripture says: 'There is a time for silence and a

time for speech.' Saviour, teach me the silence of humility, the silence of wisdom, the silence of love, the silence of perfection, the silence that speaks without words, the silence of faith.   *Translated by Barbara Greene*

PRACTICE OF SILENCE

Before prayer
[It is a helpful thing to keep a few minutes' silence before prayer, with the body relaxed and all tension gone from limbs, joints, hands, face, with the mind stilled and quiet, the attention focused on God and the heart lifted in love. Then the concerns of mind and heart can be expressed to God, either in words or continued silence.]

AFTER READING THE BIBLE

[It is helpful to keep silence so that the incident described or the teaching recorded may make its own impact on us. The Spirit of God, communing with the human spirit, can make the passage relevant to our own situation and suggest any change in attitude or initiative in action.]

WHEN WORDS ARE INADEQUATE

[The movement within the soul and our experience of God can never be adequately described in thoughts and words. Often we feel the need to voice them in some way. At other times we can do little more than short exclamations of worship – 'O God, my God!', 'O God, thou art!', 'Blessed be thou, O Christ, my Lord'.]

The mind can rise to God quicker than the voice, the spirit is anterior to the thought, and reaches God in a timeless moment.

60. GUIDANCE

Jesus promised that his Spirit would guide his disciples into all truth, both truth of mind and direction of life. There can be no hesitation in the choice between what is good and what is evil, what is loving and what is selfish, what is true and what is false. Sometimes, however, the choice is between two goods or between two paths neither of which is completely good. How do we seek the Spirit's guidance?

INSIGHTS FROM SCRIPTURE

An inner law
I will put my law within them, and I will write it upon their hearts; and I will be their God, and they shall be my people.
Jeremiah 31 : 33

Pathfinding
Your ears shall hear a word behind you, saying, 'This is the way, walk in it,' when you turn to the right hand or when you turn to the left.
Isaiah 30 : 21

Simultaneous answer
Before they call I will answer, while they are yet speaking I will hear.
Isaiah 65 : 24

Decision-making
For it has seemed good to the Holy Spirit and to us.
Acts 15 : 28

OTHER INSIGHTS

Conditions for being shown God's will
1. Readiness to accept and do God's will without any conditions or reservations.

2. Reference to God of all the problems, attitudes, opportunities and decisions of our lives.

3. Readiness to receive insights from others but not to let them decide for us.

4. Examination of any intuitions to discover any ulterior motives or reluctance.

5. Patient waiting upon God until a persistent feeling of oughtness comes.

6. Quiet putting into practice of the guidance received without dithering or looking back.

PRAYERS

Grace to ask for guidance
O God, by whom the meek are guided in judgement, and light riseth up in darkness for the godly: grant us, in all our doubts and uncertainties, the grace to ask what thou wouldest have us to do; that the Spirit of wisdom may save us from all false choices, and that in thy light we may see light, and in thy straight path may not stumble; through Jesus Christ our Lord.   *William Bright*

In times of doubts and questionings
In times of doubts and questionings, when our belief is perplexed by new learning, new teaching, new thought, when our faith is strained by Creeds, by doctrines, by mysteries beyond our understanding, give us the faithfulness of learners and the courage of believers in thee; give us boldness to examine and faith to trust all truth; patience and insight to master difficulties; stability to hold fast our tradition, with enlightened interpretation to admit all fresh truth made known to us, and in times of trouble, to grasp new knowledge really and to combine it loyally and honestly with the old; alike from stubborn rejection of new revelations, and from hasty assurance that we are wiser than our fathers, save us and help us, we humbly beseech thee, O Lord.   *Bishop Ridding's Litany*

A guiding star
O God, we need a star by which to set our journey through the world. Help us to see in the baby born at Bethlehem the eternal star which will lead us to the place where truth and love and mercy meet, so that we may kneel with shepherds and kings and find heart's joy and heart's peace in Jesus Christ.

Footmarks ahead also
Guide our feet into the way of peace, for in our confusion we do not know which way to turn, in the babel of voices we hear no clear word, in the mass of propaganda we cannot sift the truth. Give us direction in which to move, and when we cannot find it, guide our feet by thy wisdom, if unperceived by our understanding. Keep our hearts peaceful in trust, give us quiet courage, keep us steady under criticism or opposition, with unfailing love towards all, and eager expectation to see the footmarks of thy dear Son ahead, perhaps only a step or two at a time, but pointing to the peace of thy will, O Creator and Redeemer of all.

O send out thy light and thy truth; let them lead me, let them bring me to thy holy hill and to thy dwelling!
Psalm 43:3

61. RENEWAL

The first disciples remarked on the vitality of Jesus and his ability to keep going, with patience and love, under the pressure of human need. He promised that they should share these inner resources of the Spirit. He makes the same promise to his disciples today, so that we too may have sufficient vitality for our own needs and duties, and an overflow from which others may find refreshment and re-creation.

INSIGHTS FROM SCRIPTURE

Invitation
Come to me, all who labour and are heavy laden and I will
give you rest.   *Matthew 11 : 28*

A never-failing spring
Whoever drinks of the water that I shall give him will never
thirst; the water that I shall give him will become in him a
spring of water welling up to eternal life.   *John 4 : 14*

Strength received
They that wait upon the Lord shall renew their strength;
they shall mount up with wings as eagles; they shall run,
and not be weary; they shall walk, and not faint.
                                                   Isaiah 40 : 31

For the nations also
Then he showed me the river of the water of life, bright as
crystal, flowing from the throne of God and of the Lamb
through the middle of the street of the city; also, on either
side of the river, the tree of life with its twelve kinds of fruit,
yielding its fruit each month; and the leaves of the tree were
for the healing of the nations.   *Revelation 22 : 1–2*

OTHER INSIGHTS

Time needed for renewal
We cannot expect re-creation of spirit with just a passing
thought of our Lord's promises or a quick prayer that costs
little. We must take enough time to allow our Lord to put
his words into action: relax body and mind, let down all
tension and effort, rest upon him, and let his peace and
strength flow into our tired being, not wanting anything
but his wise and loving will.

A thought is enough

> Discouraged in the work of life,
>   Disheartened by its load,
> Shamed by its failures and its fears,
>   I sink beside the road;
> But only let me think of thee,
>   And then new hope springs up in me.
>
> S. Longfellow

Let God take over

When we get thoroughly tired and find ourselves in an 'impasse' it is better not to go on trying to think. It is better to make the mind follow the heart to God, as the heart has before followed the mind. When we find we can no longer think for ourselves, we can turn to him, and often he will think for us, making things clear we know not how, drawing us to obvious conclusions, we know not by what arguments, creating certainty, and satisfaction, and courage, when everything we did for ourselves only left us vague, and doubting, and not wholly convinced; not so convinced, at least, as to make conviction lead to action.

Archbishop Goodier

PRAYERS

The thirsting spirit

O Lord, I am tired and dry, a piece of ground where no water is. O Lord, if there cannot fall a dew of grace, let a spring of water rise from the depth. And if there be no spring, let me wait like the thirsty earth, until the rains break and new life springs up again.

Renewal for service

O my God, grant that I may so wait upon thee, that when quick decision and action are needed I may mount up with wings as an eagle; and when under direction of thy will and the needs of men I have to keep going under pressure, I may run and not be weary; and in times of ordinary routine and humble duty I may walk and not faint. For all my fresh springs are in thee, O God of my strength.

Renewal in the Church
O God of unchangeable power and eternal light, look favourably on thy whole Church, that wonderful and sacred mystery; and by the tranquil operation of thy perpetual providence, carry out the work of man's salvation; and let the whole world feel and see that things which were cast down are being raised up, that those which had grown old are being made new, and that all things are returning to perfection, through him from whom they took their origin, even Jesus Christ thy Son our Lord.   *Gelasian Sacramentary*

All my fresh springs are in thee, O Lord my God.

62. RESURRECTION NOW

Jesus did not promise to men simply life after death, but a quality of life now. He promised us eternal life, the sharing of God's life, participation in his own risen life. He said that he had come to give men abundant life – sufficient to keep the body in health and strength, to illuminate and guide the mind, to bring peace to the heart. If we have that life within us now, we shall not worry about our last migration into the spiritual world, for we shall know a good deal about it already.

INSIGHTS FROM SCRIPTURE

Resurrection in Christ
If any one is in Christ, he is a new creation; the old has passed away, behold, the new has come.

2 Corinthians 5: 17

Evidence of resurrection
We know that we have passed out of death into life, because
we love the brethren.   *1 John 3:14*

Living in a new dimension
If then you have been raised with Christ, seek the things
that are above, where Christ is, seated at the right hand of
God.   *Colossians 3:1*

Our commonwealth is in heaven.   *Philippians 3:20*

God here, now
Behold, I make all things new . . . a new heaven and a new
earth . . . death shall be no more, neither . . . mourning, nor
crying, nor pain . . . (for) the dwelling of God is with men.
                                        Revelation 21:5, 1, 4, 3

OTHER INSIGHTS

Everything luminous
Though the phenomena of the lower world remain the
same – the material determinisms, the vicissitudes of chance,
the laws of labour, the agitations of men, the footfalls of
death – he who *dares* to believe reaches a sphere of created
reality in which things, while retaining their habitual
texture, seem to be made out of a different substance.
Everything remains the same so far as phenomena are
concerned, but at the same time everything becomes
luminous, animated, loving . . .   *Teilhard de Chardin*

Everything new
The need for a new heart, new eyes, new patterns of judgement, and expectation – a new centre, a new goal, a new
mood, a new striving, a new commitment.   *Paul Minear*

Available now
Eternal life is not just everlasting life, a continuation of
what goes on at present, for that might not be too joyful for

many people. It is a quality of life, the kind of life which Jesus had, human life permeated by the grace and love of God, and so invulnerable to physical death. Jesus taught his disciples that they could have eternal life now, just as in the teaching of the Buddha the sphere of bliss and blessing which he called Nirvana can be enjoyed now. The perfection of both will come in the dimension beyond death.

PRAYERS

Eternity now
O feed my heart's longing! Strengthen and confirm my love; that the eternal may swallow up the temporal even now; and in that last hour I may stand before thee, sorry, ashamed, trembling, but in hope.   *Eric Milner-White*

Take death in our stride
O Christ, my Lord, thou hast promised that they who trust in thee shall never *see* death – they will hardly notice it. Thou hast also promised that they shall never *taste* death – they will hardly feel it, so great will be thy life within them that they will take it in their stride. Come within my being, O Lord of life, that I may share thy resurrection now.

A new world
O Eternal God, with thy life within me I am transformed, with quiet trust, with growing love, seeing life as a joyful adventure. I look out on the world through new eyes, seeing wonder and beauty in every created thing. I see my fellow-men no longer as rivals for the things I want or obstacles to my own advancement but as friends and brothers. I see death as my final birth into the sphere of the eternal, which I have already glimpsed and tasted through my touch with thee, O Blessed and Beloved One.

Blessed be thou, O Lord, who even now dost allow us to taste the powers and joys of the world to come, blessed for ever.

63. WORSHIP

The word 'worship' comes from an old English word meaning worthship – giving to God his true worth as Creator, Redeemer, and indwelling Spirit. Worship is man's response to these divine activities. As we realize the greatness, the goodness and the 'allness' of God, we forget ourselves and our hearts break forth in praise. Yet worship is not just the expression in words or music of feeling, but the outgoing of our hearts and the acceptance of God as the governing reality of our lives. He becomes our chiefest good and our lives are henceforth offered to him in loving obedience.

INSIGHTS FROM SCRIPTURE

The worship of heaven
Holy, holy, holy is the Lord of hosts; the whole earth is full of his glory.   *Isaiah 6 : 3*

Worthy art thou, our Lord and God, to receive glory and honour and power, for thou didst create all things, and by thy will they existed and were created.   *Revelation 4 : 11*

In the Sinai desert
Put off your shoes from your feet, for the place on which you are standing is holy ground.   *Exodus 3 : 5*

In the human heart
Thou art my Lord, I have no good apart from thee.
                                                                Psalm 16 : 2

OTHER INSIGHTS

Response to God
Worship is the submission of all our nature to God. It is the quickening of conscience by his holiness; the nourishment

of mind with his truth; the purifying of the imagination by
his beauty; the opening of the heart to his love; the surrender of will to his purpose – and all of this gathered
up in adoration, the most selfless emotion of which our
nature is capable and therefore the chief remedy of that
self-centredness which is our original sin and the source of
all actual sin.   *William Temple*

Lost in God

To adore . . . That means to lose oneself in the unfathom-
able, to plunge into the inexhaustible, to find peace in the
incorruptible, to be absorbed in defined immensity, to offer
oneself to the fire and the transparency, to annihilate oneself in proportion as one becomes more deliberately conscious of oneself, and to give of one's deepest to that whose
depth has no end.   *Teilhard de Chardin*

The soul's amen

I heard it all, I heard the whole
Harmonious hymn of being roll
Up through the chapel of my soul
And at the altar die,
And in the awful quiet then
Myself I heard, Amen, Amen,
Amen I heard me cry!   *Ralph Hodgson*

PRAYERS

A Muslim mystic's prayer

O my Lord! If I worship thee from fear of hell, burn me in
hell: if I worship thee from hope of paradise, exclude me
thence; but if I worship thee for thine own sake, then
withhold not from me thine eternal beauty.
                           Rabia of Jerusalem, c. 800 A.D.

Holy ground everywhere

O God, I see signs of thy presence in every activity of men, expressions of beauty in the arts of men, principles of truth in the sciences of men, marks of nobility in ordinary lives.

O God, I see signs of thy presence in every place, in every bush, in every creature.

Thou art indeed the fount of truth, the first author of beauty, the source of love, the Creator and Father of all, from all eternity to all eternity, ever the unchanging self from whom our lesser selves derive, in whom they find their source and goal.

Glory be to thee O God eternal.

Gloria
Glory be to thee, O Lord God, in the mystery of thy being, in the creation of the universe and in the evolution of man, in thine incarnation in Jesus Christ, in the availability of thy Spirit for every man, in all the truth, love and goodness that we find in the world, in thy truth upon our souls and in thy will for mankind. Glory to thee, O Lord most high.

We praise thee, we bless thee, we worship thee, we glorify thee, we give thanks to thee for thy great glory, O Lord God, heavenly King, God the Father Almighty.

Book of Common Prayer

X. IN THE END

*What can be thought and said about the ultimate things
of personal life and divine history?*

64. TIME

The word 'time' is used in two ways in the New Testament.
The first is in the sense of duration, time by the clock or the
calendar, a purely impersonal, chronological idea. The
second is judged by rightness, ripeness, achievement of
purpose, which is determined by reference to God, in his
goodwill, in his love and patience. Those who believe in
God try to live their lives in chronological time with ever-
deepening understanding of God's purpose, God's timeliness
and their own keen eye for opportunity.

INSIGHTS FROM SCRIPTURE

Our Lord's discrimination
My hour has not yet come . . . My time has not yet come,
but your time is always here . . . My time has not yet fully
come . . . his hour had not yet come . . . Jesus knew that
his hour had come . . . Father, the hour has come.
                    John 2:4, 7:6, 7:8, 7:30, 13:1, 17:1

A day at a time
Therefore do not be anxious about tomorrow, for tomorrow
will be anxious for itself. Let the day's own trouble be
sufficient for the day.   *Matthew 6:34*

Every day potential
Behold, now is the acceptable time; behold, now is the day
of salvation.   *2 Corinthians 6:2*

Every day available
Jesus Christ is the same yesterday and today and for ever.
                    Hebrews 13:8

OTHER INSIGHTS

Past, present, future
There are three ways of understanding time – present-
mindedness, retrospection and foresight . . . Hindsight is
used to correct foresight, but, first, hindsight must be
corrected by insight.　　　　　　　　　　*Paul Minear*

Akbar's insight
Jesus, on whom be peace, has said:
> The world is a bridge.
> Pass over it.
> But build not your dwelling there.

*Inscription on the great Mosque
in Fateh-pur-Sikri near Delhi*

Material for the spiritual life
Teach me, O God, so to use all the circumstances of my life
today that they may bring forth in me the fruits of holiness
rather than the fruits of sin.
Let me use disappointment as material for patience:
Let me use success as material for thankfulness:
Let me use suspense as material for perseverance:
Let me use danger as material for courage:
Let me use reproach as material for long suffering:
Let me use praise as material for humility:
Let me use pleasures as material for temperance:
Let me use pains as material for endurance.

– John Baillie

PRAYERS

Time to stand and stare
O God who hast revealed thyself to us not only as truth but
also as beauty, restrain us from that rude and careless haste
which disregards the manifold and incessant beauty of thy
creation, whereby thou art revealing thyself to us: grant us

the recollectedness whereby we may look on these manifest and unceasing revelations of the loveliness of thy nature and, so looking upon these reflections of thee, may begin to learn what thy unveiled splendour must be, thy formless beauty, of which all beauty of form is but a shadow.

Gerald Heard

Through the temporal

O God, the protector of all that trust in thee, without whom nothing is strong, nothing is holy; increase and multiply upon us thy mercy; that, thou being our ruler and guide, we may so pass through things temporal, that we finally lose not the things eternal: grant this, O heavenly Father, for Jesus Christ's sake our Lord. *Book of Common Prayer*

Redeeming the time

O Lord God of time and eternity, who makest us creatures of time that, when time is over, we may attain thy blessed eternity: with time, thy gift, give us also wisdom to redeem the time, lest our day of grace be lost; for our Lord Jesus' sake. *Christina Georgina Rossetti*

For any kind of evening

Abide with us, O Lord, for it is toward evening and the day is far spent; abide with us, and with thy whole Church. Abide with us in the evening of the day, in the evening of life, in the evening of the world. Abide with us and with all thy faithful ones, O Lord, in time and eternity.

Lutheran Manual of Prayer

Blessed be the hour, O Christ, in which thou wast born, and the hour in which thou didst die:
Blessed be the dawn of thy rising again, and the high day of thine ascending.
O most merciful and mighty Redeemer Christ, let all times be the time of our presence with thee, and of thy dwelling in us.

65. ETERNITY

Men have become accustomed to think of time as a fourth dimension of life, additional to the dimensions of space. The Bible tells us of a still further dimension, that of eternity. This is not just an extension of time in the sense of 'everlasting', but a new dimension, a new quality of life, which we can begin to have now, which is not terminated by physical death, and which will reach its perfection in the spiritual sphere. We Christians learn about this kind of life from Jesus Christ; more than that, he shares his own victorious, deathless life with all who will open their being to his Spirit.

Known in the divine life
This is eternal life, that they know thee the only true God, and Jesus Christ whom thou hast sent.   *John 17:3*

New sight needed
We look not to the things that are seen but to the things that are unseen; for the things that are seen are transient, but the things that are unseen are eternal.   *2 Corinthians 4:18*

The eternal city
Here we have no lasting city, but we seek the city which is to come . . . the city which has foundations, whose builder and maker is God.   *Hebrews 13:14; 11:10*

A foretaste already
For it is impossible to restore again to repentance those who have once been enlightened, who have tasted the heavenly gift, and have become partakers of the Holy Spirit, and have tasted the goodness of the word of God and the powers of the age to come.   *Hebrews 6:4–5*

OTHER INSIGHTS

Eternity now

Sometimes when we are silent before God, with outside noises unheard and the traffic of our minds stilled, then come moments of full awareness, timeless moments no longer under the domination of space and time, a direct apprehension of reality, with a quiet peace in which time seems to stand still. At other times there is a sense of holding a bucket under a waterfall, with God pouring into our souls such immediate clarity, apprehension and intuition, that our conscious minds can only retain a fraction of what we have felt and heard.

The invisible world

When we find ourselves after long rest gifted with fresh powers, vigorous with the seed of eternal life within us, able to love God as we wish, conscious that all trouble, sorrow, pain, anxiety, bereavement is over for ever, blessed in the full affection of those earthly friends whom we loved so poorly, and could protect so feebly, while they were with us in the flesh, and above all visited by the immediate visible ineffable Presence of God Almighty, with his only-begotten Son our Lord Jesus Christ, and his co-equal, co-eternal Spirit, that great sight in which is the fullness of joy and pleasure for evermore – what deep, incommunicable, unimaginable thoughts will be then upon us! What depths will be stirred up within us! What secret harmonies awaked, of which human nature seemed incapable!

John Henry Newman

When I meet God

 In the castle of my soul there is a little postern gate
 Where, when I enter, I am in the presence of God.
 In a moment, in a turning of a thought,
 I am where God is.
 When I meet God there, all life gains a new meaning,

Small things become great, and great things small.
Lowly and despised things are shot through with glory.
My troubles seem but pebbles on the road,
My joys seem like the everlasting hills,
All my fever is gone in the great peace of God,
And I pass through the door from Time into Eternity.

Walter Rauschenbusch

PRAYERS

The heart's direction

Grant us, O Lord, not to set our hearts on earthly things,
but to love things heavenly; even now, while we are placed
among things that are passing away, to cleave to those that
shall abide.   *Pope Leo I (440–461)*

The divine touch

O Lord, let me be content that I have felt thy touch upon
my spirit. Let me not presume to think that I can hold thee
within the limits of my mind or express thee fully in my
words. Rather let my whole bearing witness that thou hast
touched me.

To be continued

O God, thou hast given me flashes of understanding,
glimpses of eternity, hints which can only be followed by
guesses. Let me follow the hint half guessed, the gift half
understood, keeping faithful in prayer, discipline and
obedience, until you make your presence felt again and
lead me into deeper knowledge, truer truth, more loving
love, timeless peace and union with thee, O Blessed and
Eternal One.

Prepared and waiting

Things beyond our seeing, things beyond our hearing,
things beyond our imagining, all prepared by God for those
who love him.   *1 Corinthians 2:9 (NEB)*

66. JUDGEMENT

People often wonder about the end of the world and the consummation of human life. Conscience reminds us of past wrongs, foolish actions and childish ignorances. Scripture and preachers remind us of a judgement to come and some people are unscriptural enough to claim to predict the day and hour. The secret is to see ourselves in the light of God's holiness and love, to acknowledge our need of forgiveness, to accept God's forgiveness and his grace, so that when death or judgement comes we may be ready, trusting and unafraid.

INSIGHTS FROM SCRIPTURE

When?
Of that day or hour no one knows, not even the angels in heaven, nor the Son, but only the Father. Take heed, watch; for you do not know when the time will come.
Mark 13:32–33

No secrets hidden
Before him no creature is hidden, but all are open and laid bare to the eyes of him with whom we have to do.
Hebrews 4:13

An understanding judge
For we have not a high priest who is unable to sympathize with our weaknesses, but one who in every respect has been tempted as we are, yet without sin. *Hebrews 4:15*

Angels, saints, sinners – and Jesus
But you have come to Mount Zion and to the city of the living God, the heavenly Jerusalem, and to innumerable angels in festal gathering, and to the assembly of the first-born who are enrolled in heaven, and to a judge who is God of all, and to the spirits of just men made perfect, and to

Jesus, the mediator of a new covenant, and to the sprinkled blood that speaks more graciously than the blood of Abel.

Hebrews 12 : 22–24

OTHER INSIGHTS

Books of judgement

In the book of Revelation St John sees in vision the dead standing before God and being judged from books of record These books are not the book of life, for that is mentioned separately. It has been suggested that they are the books of memory and character.

Self-knowledge

True self-knowledge will not just be the recollection of past sins, failures and weaknesses, though that will be painful enough. It will be the realization of how far short even our best falls, the recognition perhaps for the first time of our secret motives. This is an exercise which needs to be under·taken now, and regularly, in the light of God's awe-ful holiness, and of our own need of Christification.

Self-judgement

It will not be a case of a puzzled anxious prisoner in the dock waiting in trepidation to hear the verdict of the judge, but one who judges himself. To see burning holiness and then to look at one's own pitiful selfishness and uncleanness, will make one cry out with Isaiah 'Woe is me!' To see perfect love and then to look at one's own mean, miserly soul, will need no verdict and sentence. I shall know: my only hope lies in the fact that judgement has been committed to our Lord, and he is Saviour as well as Lord.

PRAYERS

A cry for help
  Come down, O Christ, and help me! reach thy hand,
      For I am drowning in a stormier sea
      Than Simon on thy lake of Galilee:
  The wine of life is spilt upon the sand,
  My heart is as some famine-murdered land
      Whence all good things have perished utterly,
      And well I know my soul in Hell must lie
  If I this night before God's throne should stand.

Oscar Wilde

Not blameless but forgiven
Withhold not from me, O my God, the best, the Spirit of
thy dear Son; that in that day when the judgement is set I
may be presented unto thee not blameless, but forgiven,
not effectual but faithful, not holy but persevering, without
desert but accepted, because he hath pleaded the causes of
my soul, and redeemed my life.   *Eric Milner-White*

Nightly judgement
Grant, O Lord, that each day before I enter the little death
of sleep, I may undergo the little judgement of the past day,
so that every wrong deed may be forgiven and every un-
holy thought set right. Let nothing go down into the depths
of my being which has not been forgiven and sanctified.
Then I shall be ready for my final birth into eternity and
look forward with hope and love to standing before thee,
who art both judge and Saviour, holy judge and loving
Saviour.

We believe that thou shalt come to be our judge. We therefore pray thee help thy servants whom thou hast redeemed
with thy precious blood. Make us to be numbered with thy
saints in glory everlasting.   *Te Deum*

67. COMPLETING THE UNIVERSE

Astronomers tell us that galaxies of stars are still being brought into existence millions of light years away in infinite space. Evidently creation is still going on. Natural catastrophes still take place, the causes of which have still to be discovered. For the present, incurable diseases take toll of many lives. Clearly there are flaws in the universe that need to be set right or avoided. Men now have the ability to alter the course of rivers, to build dams, to irrigate deserts, desalinate sea water. Modern man can co-operate with God in completing the universe, in a way of which previous generations had no idea.

INSIGHTS FROM SCRIPTURE

Birthpangs of a new order
These things are the beginning of travail (wars, upheavals, widespread suffering and fear). *Mark 13 : 8* (RV)

Signs of the coming Kingdom
When these things begin to come to pass, look up, and lift up your heads; because your redemption draweth nigh.
Luke 21 : 28 (RV)

A delayed birth
We know that the whole creation has been groaning in travail together until now. *Romans 8 : 22*

Men must co-operate
For the creation waits with eager longing for the revealing of the sons of God. *Romans 8 : 19*

The end is assured
Then comes the end, when Christ delivers the kingdom to

God the Father after destroying every rule and every
authority and power.   *1 Corinthians 15:24*

OTHER INSIGHTS

The prophet's vision
In the book of Isaiah there are three passages describing the
messianic age. It will comprise a ruler inspired by the
Spirit of the Lord, governing in righteousness. It will be an
age of plenty with the desert blossoming with flowers. Man
will live in harmony with the animals. The physically
handicapped will be enabled to overcome their handicaps.
It will be nothing less than the transformation of the
universe, the abolition of all sorrow, all frustration of effort,
all violence and premature death. It will be an age of peace,
in God's perfecting of the world.
                    Isaiah 11:1–9, 35:1–10, 65:17–25

Where to start
Every man, in the course of his life, must not only show
himself obedient and docile. By his fidelity he must build –
starting with the most natural territory of his own self – a
work . . . into which something enters from all the elements
of the earth. He makes his own soul throughout all his
earthly days; and at the same time he collaborates in another work, which infinitely transcends . . . the perspectives
of his individual achievement: the completing of the world.
                    Teilhard de Chardin

When to start
How wonderful it is that nobody need wait a single moment
before beginning to improve the world.
                    Anne Frank (the fourteen-year-old girl, just
                    before being dragged off to her death in 1944)

One great day of victory
              This day relenting God
              Hath placed within my hand

A wondrous thing; and God
  Be praised. At his command

Seeking his secret deeds
  With tears and toiling breath,
I find thy cunning seeds,
  O million murdering death.

I know this little thing
  A myriad men will save.
O death, where is thy sting?
  Thy victory, O grave?

> *Sir Ronald Ross* (on the day
> when he proved to his satis-
> faction the connection between
> the mosquito and malaria)

PRAYERS

Divine discontent

O Lord, we pray thee that thou wilt hasten the time when
no man shall live in contentment while he knows that others
have need. Inspire in us and in men of all nations the desire
for social justice, that the hungry may be fed, the homeless
welcomed, the sick healed, and a just and peaceful order
established in the world, according to thy gracious will
made known in Jesus Christ, our Lord.

'Incurables'?

O Heavenly Father, we pray thee for those suffering from
diseases for which at present there is no cure. Give them the
victory of trust and hope, that they may never lose their
faith in thy loving purpose. Grant thy wisdom to all who are
working to discover the secrets of disease, and the faith that
through thee all things are possible. We ask this in the name
of him who went about doing good and healing all kinds of
disease, even thy Son Jesus Christ our Lord.

United in the new creation

O God, who hast made of one blood all nations of the earth and didst send thy blessed Son to be the redeemer of all mankind: unite us in our common humanity and make us one new man in the same thy Son, Jesus Christ, our Lord.

Quickly, Lord Jesus!

O blessed Lord, I pray with you your own prayer 'Thy Kingdom come, thy will be done, on earth as it is in heaven.' Let it happen quickly, O Lord Jesus.

68. UNCEASING PURPOSE

Scientists tell us that matter has been in existence for over a thousand million years. Throughout that near eternal age of time God has been at work with unfailing wisdom and patience, taming the recalcitrance of matter, enabling each species of life to find its own goal of beauty and usefulness, training men in mind and spirit, drawing them together in unity, and in Jesus Christ showing them the prototype of human maturity as well as the image of divine love. We know from his revelation of himself that his purpose is good, loving, wise, the most effective thing to be done in every situation, and that his creative and redemptive work will continue until his eternal purpose is achieved.

INSIGHTS FROM SCRIPTURE

Discovering God's will

Do not be conformed to this world but be transformed by the renewal of your mind, that you may prove what is the will of God, what is good and acceptable and perfect.

Romans 12 : 2

Energy from God's will

My food is to do the will of him who sent me, and to accomplish his work.

John 4 : 34

Trusting God's will
Father, if thou art willing, remove this cup from me;
nevertheless not my will, but thine, be done.   *Luke 22:42*

Expressing God's will
The wisdom from above is first pure, then peaceable,
gentle, open to reason, full of mercy and good fruits, without
uncertainty or insincerity.   *James 3:17*

OTHER INSIGHTS

Overflow of love
The disciples ask Jesus whether a man had been born blind
because of his own sin, or his parents', or whose. Our Lord
replies that it cannot be traced either to the man himself or to
his parents, and puts aside as irrelevant the whole question of
finding the culprit. 'Can't you see,' he says in effect, 'that
here is a piece of God's work waiting to be done? The
important thing is to recognize it and do it, and not waste
time and energy in seeking for someone to blame.' He then
takes it on himself to give the time and energy required to
make the blind man's suffering the occasion for an overflow
of love in a work of healing mercy.

Professor Leonard Hodgson

Marks of God's will

> Holiness
> Love
> Sacrifice
> Relevance
> Newness

A dynamic force
God's will is not just goodwill towards men in the sense of a
benevolent disposition, though it is certainly that. It is a
determined, dynamic force, working to achieve his purpose,
ceaselessly opposed to evil, constantly countering the mistaken or sinful moves of men, always ready to guide those

who take his will as the purpose of their lives, immediately generous to supply more than abundant grace to carry it out. 'Thy will be done!' is a cry of glad acceptance of the rightness, goodness and love of God. 'Thy will be done' is an equally joyful conviction.

PRAYERS

Nothing could be better
Thy will be done: so good, so holy, so loving, so wise, so effective. Thy will be done!

God knows the better way
O Lord God, when we pray unto thee, desiring well and meaning truly, if thou seest a better way to thy glory and our good, then be thy will done, and not ours: as with thy dear Son in the garden of Agony, even Jesus Christ our Lord.
Eric Milner-White

Made and redeemed for God's will
O Lord Jesu Christ, who hast made me and redeemed me and brought me where I am upon my way: thou knowest what thou wouldst do with me; do with me according to thy will, for thy tender mercies' sake.   *Henry VI*

On earth
O God, I thank thee that thy will is love instead of hatred, health instead of disease, life instead of death, plenty instead of hunger, peace instead of war, freedom instead of oppression, decent houses instead of slums, caring communities instead of concentration camps, refugee camps, prisons, heaven instead of hell. I know that thou wilt never cease thy eternal purpose of love until thy Kingdom comes on earth as in heaven, and thy will be done by men as well as by angels and saints. Blessed be thou, good God!

Lo, I come to fulfil thy will, O my God. I delight to do it, for thy law is within my heart, O my God.   *Psalm 40: 10*

69. TO THE END

Every life has its own temptations, difficulties and problems, but equally its own joys, adventures and opportunities. Most of us in the course of our lifetime will have learned something of the meaning of life and have grown in maturity, enough at any rate to want to continue. Our trust for what lies beyond this life is the faith that the God who has created us will not destroy us just as we are beginning to reach some maturity, or even if we have failed to do so. The circumstances of our birth, and the happenings of life, and the character we have, are the raw material with which we build for the future, aided by God's unfailing grace.

INSIGHTS FROM SCRIPTURE

The ultimate aim
That I may know him and the power of his resurrection, and may share his sufferings, becoming like him in his death, that if possible I may attain the resurrection from the dead. *Philippians 3 : 10–11*

The ultimate goal
One thing I do, forgetting what lies behind and straining forward to what lies ahead, I press on toward the goal for the prize of the upward call of God in Christ Jesus.
Philippians 3 : 13–14

The ultimate strength
Who is sufficient for these things? . . . our competence is from God . . . 'My grace is sufficient for you, for my power is made perfect in weakness.' *2 Corinthians 2 : 16, 3 : 5, 12 : 9*

The ultimate hope
For I know whom I have believed, and I am sure that he is able to guard until that Day what has been entrusted to me.

2 Timothy 1:12

OTHER INSIGHTS

Victory assured
He said not: Thou shalt not be tempested, thou shalt not be travailed, thou shalt not be afflicted; but he said: Thou shalt not be overcome. *Mother Julian of Norwich*

Re-union assured

It matters not, when I am dead,
    Where this dull clay shall lie,
Nor what the dogmas, creeds and rites
    Decree to us who die.

I only know that I shall tread
    The paths my dead have trod,
And where the hearts I love have gone,
    There I shall find my God.

Kendall Banning

The final offering
On the day when death will knock at my door what shall I offer him, either in the closing minutes of this life or in the opening minutes of my new birth in the life beyond? Oh, I will set before him all the lovely things that I have seen, all the love that I have received and given, all the insights of truth that I have gathered, all the things that I have valued and enjoyed, all the tasks completed or left for others, all my gratitude and love for the past, all my content in the present and my hope for the future. Above all I will offer my recognition of the Lord who has come in the guise of death, to lead me to the home he has prepared for me.

Inspired by *Rabindranath Tagore*

Gifts which create the future
Lord of all power and might, who art the author and giver
of all good things: graft in our hearts the love of thy name,
increase in us true religion, nourish us with all goodness,
and of thy great mercy keep us in the same; through Jesus
Christ our Lord.   *Book of Common Prayer*

With God all the way
Go before us, O Lord, in all our doings with thy most
gracious favour, and further us with thy continual help; that
in all our works, begun, continued, and ended in thee, we
may glorify thy holy name, and finally by thy mercy obtain
everlasting life; through Jesus Christ our Lord.
                                        Book of Common Prayer

Keeping nothing back
Take, Lord, all my liberty. Receive my memory, my understanding and my whole will. Whatever I have and possess
thou hast given to me; to thee I restore it wholly, and to thy
will I utterly surrender it for thy direction. Give me the
love of thee only, with thy grace, and I am rich enough;
nor ask I anything beside.   *Ignatius Loyola*

Gloria
Now to him who is able to keep you from falling and to
present you without blemish before the presence of his glory
with rejoicing, to the only God, our Saviour through Jesus
Christ our Lord, be glory, majesty, dominion, and authority, before all time and now and for ever. Amen.   *Jude 24*

The Bible opens with the words 'In the beginning God . . .'; it could very well close in actual words, as it does in meaning, 'In the end God . . .' If the spirit in man came from God, as Jews, Muslims and Christians believe, then it will return to God. In my beginning is the seed of my end; in my end is the fulfilment of my beginning:

INSIGHTS FROM SCRIPTURE

This is eternal life, that they know thee the only true God, and Jesus Christ whom thou hast sent. *John 17:3*

Pilgrims of faith
They desire a better country, that is, a heavenly one. Therefore God is not ashamed to be called their God, for he has prepared for them a city. *Hebrews 11:16*

The supreme value
Whom have I in heaven but thee? And there is nothing upon earth that I desire besides thee. *Psalm 73:25*

The sure way
You shall love the Lord your God with all your heart, and with all your soul, and with all your mind, and with all your strength. *Mark 12:30* (from Deuteronomy 6:5)

PRAYERS

How easy with God
How easy it is for me to live with you, Lord!
How easy it is for me to believe in you!
When my mind is distraught and my reason fails,
When the cleverest people do not see further than this evening what must be done tomorrow

You grant me the clear confidence
   that you exist, and that you will take care
   that not all the ways of goodness are stopped.
   At the height of earthly fame I gaze with wonder
   at that path through hopelessness –
   to this point from which even I have been able
   to convey to men some reflection of the Light
   which comes from you.
   And you will enable me to go on doing
   as much as needs to be done.
   And in so far as I do not manage it –
   that means that you have allotted the task to others.

Alexander Solzhenitsyn

Pearls for pearls

O God, grant that I may go on exchanging pearls for pearls,
small truths for greater truths, good things for better things,
until I come at length to the truth itself, to thee who art its
source and giver, the giver of all good and the source of all
love.

The open door

The seer of the book of Revelation noticed a door that had
been open all the time. Through it could be seen

       the slain Lamb now enthroned
       the worship of heaven
       the eternal purpose of God
       the defeat of evil
       the victory of righteousness
       the end of suffering and tears
       the angels, martyrs and saints
       a vast crowd of humble, holy souls
       the holy city of God's will
       descending to men
       the river of life
       and all things being made new.

Lord, let me look through that same door and with wonder
and hope approach it, and by thy mercy enter through it

to worship more truly, love more perfectly and live more gloriously.

Looking back

Lord, as I look back on the journey so far, I see how thy love and goodness have been with me, through many failings and dangers, in many joys and adventures. I have received much love from friends, enjoyed so many good and lovely things, been guided and inspired by the wisdom and encouragement of many teachers and writers.

Often I have felt thy presence near, and often I have had to walk by faith.

Forgive my slowness, my failures in faith, the smallness of my love, my poor use of thy grace.

Accept my heart's thanks for growing knowledge of thee, for increasing assurance of thy purposes of love and deepening knowledge of the things that are eternal. As I turn again to the journey ahead, it is bright with thy mercies of the past, dear God and Saviour.

Looking forward

There will come a time when my links with earth will grow weaker, when my powers fail, when I must bid farewell to dear ones still rooted in this life with their tasks to fulfil and their loved ones to care for, when I must detach myself from the loveliest things and begin the lonely journey. Then I shall hear the voice of my beloved Christ, saying 'It is I, be not afraid.' So with my hand in his, from the dark valley I shall see the shining City of God and climb with quiet trusting steps and be met by the Father of souls and clasped in the everlasting arms.

Blessed be God, the only God: three persons in one eternity of love. Blessed be God for all that he is. Blessed be God for all that he has done. Blessed in his Church on earth, and blessed in the height of heaven. Blessed from everlasting, blessed now, and blessed for evermore. Blessed be God.

INDEX

INDEX

Alcuin, 143

Allingham, Margery, 91, 111

Aquinas, Thomas, 20, 98

Augustine, St, 90, 110, 129, 140

Baeck, Rabbi Leo, 74

Baillie, John, 222

Banning, Kendall, 237

Bea, Cardinal, 74

Bekr, Abu, 33

Binyon, G. C., 161-2

Blanding, 54

Bonhoeffer, Dietrich, 145

Book of Common Prayer, 41, 112, 156-7, 186, 203-4, 217, 223, 238

Bright, William, 89, 208

Buber, Martin, 152

Buddha, The, 29, 65

Butterfield, Herbert, 152

Carter, Sydney, 164

Chesterton, G. K., 116

Cloud of Unknowing, The, 92, 94

Coleridge, Mary, 142-3

Conze, E., 128

Cragg, Kenneth, 200

Davis, Charles, 119

Dearmer, Percy, 161

Dietrich, Suzanne de, 106

Drake, Francis, 46

Eckhart, Meister, 24

Erasmus, Desiderius, 158

Feuerbach, Ludwig, 27

Flecker, James Elroy, 119

Frank, Anne, 231

Fuller, Thomas, 52

Gandhi, Mahatma, 152-3

Gelasian Sacramentary, 183, 212

Goodier, Archbishop, 46, 112, 191, 211

Gore, Charles, 139

Greene, Barbara, 205-6

Gregory, T. S., 128

Grey, Lady Jane, 52

Grou, J. N., 205

Hallaj, Al, 65

Hammarskjöld, Dag, 197

Harding, Geoffrey, 114

Harnack, Professor, 48

Heard, Gerald, 222-3

Henrich, Ruth, 140

Henry VI, 235

Heschel, Rabbi Abraham, 146

Higham, Florence, 63

Hodgson, Leonard, 155, 234

Hodgson, Ralph, 216

Hoskyns, E. C., 25

Hoyland, J. S., 100, 171

Hügel, Friedrich von, 137

Hujwiri, 203

Huxley, Thomas, 82

Inge, W. R., 19

Israel, Martin, 111

John of the Cross, St, 33, 92

Jung, C. G., 22, 37

Kempis, Thomas à, 20
Kingsley, Charles, 75

Leo I, Pope, 226
Lessius, Fr, 25
Longfellow, Stephen, 211
Loyola, Ignatius, 238
Lutheran Manual of Prayer,
    223

Macaulay, Rose, 86
Macdonald, George, 33, 43, 94,
    109, 182, 188
Macquarrie, John, 23, 91, 133
Marcel, Gabriel, 137
Masefield, John, 40
Masirerich, C. de, 25
Matthews, W. R., 25
Maurice, F. D., 145
Merton, Thomas, 97
Milner-White, Eric, 55-6, 78,
    84, 92, 101, 107, 109, 112,
    129, 138, 140-1, 180-1, 189,
    203, 214, 229, 235
Minear, Paul, 108, 200, 213
Mother Julian of Norwich, 52,
    131, 237
Moule, C., 100
Myers, F. W. H., 117

Neill, Stephen, 179
Nelson, J. Robert, 68
New Every Morning, 137
Newman, John Henry, 225
Niebuhr, Reinhold, 28, 101

Oldham, J. H., 27, 89, 128

Perron, Fr, 145

Punch, 51

Rabia of Jerusalem, 216
Ramsey, Michael, 77, 203
Rauschenbusch, Walter, 225-6
Reuerbach, Ludwig, 27
Richard of Chichester, St, 159
Ridding, Bishop's Litany, 208
Rideau-Emile, 27
Robin, Bishop, 167
Robinson, A. W., 41
Ross, Sir Ronald, 231-2
Rossetti, Christina Georgina,
    195-6, 223
Royce, Josiah, 179

St Michael and St George,
    Order of, 101
Sayers, Dorothy, 51
Schoeps, 142
Schweitzer, Albert, 152, 194
Scott, Lesbia, 191
Shaw, Fr Gilbert, 203
Silesius, Angelus, 37-8
Solzhenitsyn, Alexander, 239-
    40
Sorley, C. H., 139
Spens, Maisie, 158
Stevenson, Robert Louis, 87

Tagore, Rabindranath, 43, 49,
    54, 95, 237
Talmon, Professor J. L., 30
Taylor, Jeremy, 17, 156
Teilhard de Chardin, 48, 54,
    86-7, 110, 119-20, 134-5, 146,
    194-5, 213, 216, 231
Temple, William, 45, 55, 71-2,
    88, 91, 131, 134, 137, 142,
    160, 161, 215-16
Tilak, 116, 165
Tillich, Paul, 85, 176

Traherne, Thomas, 40

Underhill, Evelyn, 20, 95, 114, 179

Vaughan, Dean, 164

Warren, Max, 62-3

Weil, Simone, 89
West, Morris, 109
Wilde, Oscar, 229
Williams, H. A., 182
Wouk, Herman, 130

Zeller, Hubert van, 167, 200, 202

Also available in the Fontana Religious Series

The Divine Pity
GERALD VANN

Undoubtedly Gerald Vann's masterpiece. Many people have insisted that this book should not merely be read, but re-read constantly, for it becomes more valuable the more it is pondered upon.

The Founder of Christianity
C. H. DODD

A portrait of Jesus by the front-ranking New Testament scholar. 'A first-rate and fascinating book . . . this book is a theological event.'   *Times Literary Supplement*

Science and Christian Belief
C. A. COULSON

'Professor Coulson's book is one of the most profound studies of the relationship of science and religion that has yet been published.'   *Times Literary Supplement*

Something Beautiful for God
MALCOLM MUGGERIDGE

'For me, Mother Teresa of Calcutta embodies Christian love in action. Her face shines with the love of Christ on which her whole life is centred. *Something Beautiful for God* is about her and the religious order she has instituted.'
Malcolm Muggeridge

Jesus Rediscovered
MALCOLM MUGGERIDGE

'. . . one of the most beautifully written, perverse, infuriating, enjoyable and moving books of the year.'
David L. Edwards, Church Times

Also available in the Fontana Religious Series

Something Beautiful for God
MALCOLM MUGGERIDGE

'For me, Mother Teresa of Calcutta embodies Christian love in action. Her face shines with the love of Christ on which her whole life is centred. *Something Beautiful for God* is about her and the religious order she has instituted.'

Malcolm Muggeridge

Instrument of Thy Peace
ALAN PATON

'Worthy of a permanent place on the short shelf of enduring classics of the life of the Spirit.'

Henry P. van Dusen, Union Theological Seminary

Sing A New Song
THE PSALMS IN TODAY'S ENGLISH VERSION

These religious poems are of many kinds: there are hymns of praise and worship of God; prayers for help, protection, and salvation; pleas for forgiveness; songs of thanksgiving for God's blessings; and petitions for the punishment of enemies. This translation of the *Psalms in Today's English Version* has the same freshness and clarity of language, the same accuracy of scholarship based on the very best originals available as *Good News for Modern Man* and *The New Testament in Today's English Version*.

The Gospel According to Peanuts
ROBERT L. SHORT

This book has made a lasting appeal to people of all denominations and none. It has been read and enjoyed by literally millions of people. A wonderfully imaginative experiment in Christian communication.

Also available in the Fontana Religious Series

The Prayer of the Universe
TEILHARD DE CHARDIN

A selection of Teilhard's most beautiful writings. This book will appeal to the thousands of readers who have read and re-read his best-sellers *Le Milieu Divin* and *Hymn of the Universe*.

To Me Personally
WILF WILKINSON

'When Wilf Wilkinson talks about the Bible, he makes it seem as though it has just been written, and not what some people think it is – 2,000 years out of date!'   *Roy Trevivian*

The Great Divorce
C. S. LEWIS

'It is all very witty, very entertaining, very readable, and Mr Lewis's fecundity of imagination is a thing to marvel at.'
                                          Roger Lloyd, Time and Tide

The Difference in Being a Christian Today
JOHN A. T. ROBINSON

'Dr Robinson is addressing himself not to the rarefied world of *haute theologie* but to men of more modest academic pretensions or of none, which he does, nevertheless without talking down. . . . His is the theology of the people and for the people.'   *Clifford Longley, The Times*

Also available in the Fontana Religious Series

How Modern Should Theology Be?
HELMUT THIELICKE

'Thielicke touches on basic theological issues for today, but he does it with such a light hand, and with such graphic powers of illustration that I really cannot recall any other modern preacher who is so much *au fait* with modern theological questions.' *Ronald Gregor Smith*

Strange Victory
GORDON W. IRESON

The Gospel, we are told, is Good News. What of? When we invite a man to become a Christian, what exactly are we offering to him, and asking him? These are some of the questions this book seeks to answer.

Companion to the Good News
JOSEPH RHYMER and ANTHONY BULLEN

More than 30 million people have bought *Good News for Modern Man* since it was first published. This 'Companion' has been written to help people understand the New Testament.

Apologia Pro Vita Sua
J. H. NEWMAN

A passionate defence of Cardinal Newman's own intellectual and spiritual integrity by a man who had been under continuous attack for many years.

Also available in the Fontana Religious Series

Double Zero
DAVID COLLYER

A fantastic story of a remarkable ministry; a story of courage, devotion and endurance to sustain and to succeed in an unorthodox ministry amongst Rockers in the city of Birmingham.

Don't Turn Me Off, Lord
CARL BURKE

'Short, pithy little essays' by the best-selling author of *God is for Real, Man.*

Where the Action Is
RITA SNOWDEN

Short sketches of interesting people from a wide variety of backgrounds: some famous and some who are not well-known. At the end of each story Rita Snowden sums up the theme in a short prayer.

The Parables of Peanuts
ROBERT L. SHORT

The Christian message is crystal clear and shows convincingly that Peanuts is essentially theological and deeply Christian.

Bible Stories
DAVID KOSSOFF

'To my mind there is no doubt that these stories make the Bible come alive. Mr Kossoff is a born story-teller. He has the gift of making the old stories new.'   *William Barclay*

Also available in the Fontana Religious Series

Children with Special Needs in the Infants' School
LESLEY WEBB

'Throughout the book the observations and reports show a deep understanding of, and regard and sympathy for, the children.'   *Teaching and Training*

Prayers for Young People
WILLIAM BARCLAY

The book includes morning and evening prayers for every week of the year, designed to help young people to pray, and also a fine introductory chapter, 'You and Your Prayers.'

The Plain Man Looks at the Bible
WILLIAM BARCLAY

This book is meant for the plain man who would like to know what to think about the Bible today. The first part deals with what the Bible is and what it is not. The second part shows that the Bible is also a record of certain things that happened.

The Bible Story
WILLIAM NEIL

'Like all his work it is hardly to be faulted, and I have never read so splendid a conspectus of the whole Bible. It will help a great many people to get their ideas sorted out. William Neil writes with such authority and lucidity that it can hardy fail.'   *J. B. Phillips*